12/15

'AY 2017

D0129927

The
Paleo Diet
HEALING BIBLE

First published in the UK in 2015 by
APPLE PRESS
74-77 White Lion Street
London N1 9PF
United Kingdom

www.apple-press.com

© 2015 Quantum Books Ltd

ISBN: 978-1-84543-616-2

Printed in China by 1010 Printing International Ltd

2 4 6 8 10 9 7 5 3 1

QUMPOHB

The
Paleo Diet
HEALING BIBLE

Christine Bailey

Contents

Introduction

Welcome to *The Paleo Diet Healing Bible*. Whether you are new to the Paleo lifestyle or are looking for inspiration to add variety to your diet, this book is for you. In this book, we have focused on providing you with detailed information about the recommended foods in a Paleo diet together with a range of healthy recipes to get you started.

The Paleo Diet Healing Bible is a fabulous resource and trusted guidebook explaining the beneficial reasons for following the Paleo diet. We have included practical strategies to ensure your food is healthy and high in valuable nutrients, which will enable you to optimize the health benefits of a Paleo diet. We also provide clear guidance on the best foods to include and – just as importantly – those to avoid.

About the Author

Christine Bailey is an award winning nutritional therapist, chef, author and broadcaster with over 18 years of experience. With a passion for creating delicious nourishing recipes, Christine has a reputation for transforming people's health and inspiring love of real food. In this book Christine combines her knowledge and scientific research in the field of functional nutrition with easy-to-follow guidance that is realistic, practical and achievable.

Living
Paleo

What is the Paleo Diet?

The Paleo diet is not simply a diet. It is a lifestyle; it involves changing the way you eat and live. It is also a personalized plan designed to find the foods that make you feel healthy and energized. The Paleo diet is more accurately described as the Paleo movement, because we know that a lot of the ill health in the Western world comes from the contemporary choices we make. We never evolved to eat refined sugar, and were never meant to spend half our lives sitting down or to live in isolation without a sense of community.

The Paleo diet was originally based on research led by the American academic Dr. Loren Cordain and others. It is a wholefood diet that includes only the most nutritionally dense, natural foods.

The thinking behind the Paleo diet focuses on our biochemical make up and the interaction of our genes and our environment. Our genetics have changed little since we lived as hunter gatherers and optimal health depends on basing our diet around food we are genetically suited to eat. The Paleo diet is based on ideas about the way we ate in the past before processed foods, sugars, salts, high-fructose corn syrups and modified produce became commonplace. The diet concentrates on foods that were available to our Paleolithic ancestors around 2.5 million years ago. Our diet and the food now available to us have changed significantly, so the diet has to be adapted to our modern lives. It makes the most of high quality, nutrient-rich foods in their natural form that are readily available today.

A Paleo diet emphasizes a high intake of a wide variety of seasonal vegetables, a moderate intake of seasonal fruit and plenty of high-quality meat, game, fish, seafood, nuts and seeds. It removes all grains, dairy products and legumes (pulses) from the diet.

Within this framework variations in the diet can be accommodated. For example, people with autoimmune-related conditions find the Paleo approach beneficial but may exclude some foods, which can promote an immune reaction and inflammation.

What Does the Paleo Diet Include?

- Organic red meats
- Wild game
- Organ meats
- Offal
- Organic poultry
- Eggs
- Fish
- Shellfish and seafood
- Fresh vegetables
- Starchy vegetables
- Sea vegetables
- Nuts
- Seeds
- Fresh fruits and berries
- Quality fats and oils (lard, duck fat plus olive, walnut, flaxseed, macadamia, avocado and coconut oil, etc.)
- Honey, stevia, coconut sugar, xylitol (okay to consume in moderation)
- Herbs and spices
- Fermented foods (kefir, sauerkraut, kombucha, etc.)
- Water, herbal teas, green and black tea (in moderation), green juices and smoothies, coconut water, nut and seed milks
- Bone broth
- Coffee (occasionally)
- Alcohol (occasionally).

What Foods Should Be Avoided?

- Grains including gluten and non-gluten grains (wheat, spelt, rye, barley, oats, corn, quinoa, rice, amaranth, millet, buckwheat, teff, wild rice, sorghum)
- Beans and pulses (including peanuts and soy)
- Dairy products (see page 28)
- Processed fatty meats (hot dogs, etc.)
- Soft drinks, fizzy drinks, fruit juice
- Sugars, syrups and artificial sweeteners
- Processed foods and ready meals
- Refined vegetable oils
- Milk and white chocolate and sweets
- Refined table salt.

Adopting the Lifestyle

While this book focuses on the food and drinks that we consume, it is important to bear in mind that the Paleo approach is a non-sedentary lifestyle – getting enough rest and relaxation, and spending time socializing in a supportive environment is equally important to your health.

The Paleo Food Pyramid

The Paleo diet is based on what our ancestors ate and how they lived, so the diet focuses on unprocessed whole food, fresh vegetables, organic meat and eggs, fish and fruit, healthy fats (including saturated fat) and cuts out dairy, refined sugars, grains, beans and processed food. The pyramid opposite shows what to include in the diet and how much of each group you should eat. For example, consume lots of fresh vegetables and organic meat, poultry, eggs and fish. Eat less fruit as it is high in natural sugars, and eat nuts and seeds in moderation as they are high in monounsaturated fats. In every meal you should try to eat some fresh vegetables and/or fruit, lean meat, nuts and seeds, and include some healthy oil.

Herbs and spices are packed with beneficial nutrients, so use them to flavour your food. In addition, spices contain zero calories, carbs, sugar, fibre, protein or fat.

Eat nuts and seeds in moderation as they are rich in monounsaturated fats. Only eat healthy fats and oils like olive oil, avocado oil, coconut oil or butter.

Eat fruits and berries that are low in sugar daily and save high-sugar fruit like bananas or mangoes for days when you need a higher carbohydrate intake.

Eat lots of organic lean meat, organic poultry and wild fresh-caught fish and seafood. Only eat moderate amounts of eggs as they are relatively high in fat.

Fresh vegetables are packed with nutrients, so eat plenty of them, especially leafy greens and non-starchy tubers and root vegetables.

Left: Consume a wide variety of fresh locally grown and seasonal produce every day.

Herbs
and
spices

Nuts, seeds,
nut butters,
healthy fats
and oils

Organic fruit

Organic, free-range meat, fish, shellfish, poultry, game and eggs

Organic locally grown vegetables

The Importance of Hydration

As part of a healthy Paleo diet it is essential to make sure you drink plenty of water, either on its own or with a tangy squeeze of lemon or lime. Drinking water can flush out toxins and improves the skin.

Making the Transition

If you are looking to adopt a Paleo diet but you don't feel ready to dive straight in, there is no reason why you cannot take your time and transition to the diet over several weeks. This may be particularly suitable if you are suffering with significant health concerns such as diabetes. You can allow yourself to switch gradually to the Paleo diet as well as increasing other key elements of a healthy lifestyle such as exercise, stress reduction and getting enough sleep.

There may be many aspects in your diet that you will need to change and doing this all at once can be too stressful. For example, if you are addicted to coffee and carbs, you may wish to eliminate one of these first, rather than both together.

One of the first priorities is to exclude grains from your diet – first focus on gluten grains (barley, rye and wheat), which are often associated with digestive problems, autoimmune diseases and inflammation. You can then start to eliminate non-gluten grains like rice, millet, quinoa and amaranth.

You can then remove dairy from your diet and switch to alternatives such as coconut and almond milk. You can create your own nut milks and nut cheeses, and can use nut milk to make ice creams and desserts (see page 197).

Clearing out your storecupboard is another good way to ensure that you follow the diet. Stop buying non-Paleo products and compost or donate other foods to food banks or to friends who are not Paleo.

For many people the reduction in carbohydrates is the most difficult part of the diet. People respond differently to the reduction in carbohydrates. Initially, you might feel sluggish or foggy-headed. Reduce your intake over time and make sure you include enough medium-chain triglycerides (fatty acids), like coconut oil, which the body can readily use as an energy source to avoid fatigue.

Get Support and Stay Motivated

Keep a food/exercise/stress management journal to track your progress. There are also many free apps which can help you to monitor your dietary intake and mood. In addition to noting down the foods eaten, recording how you feel can be very motivating and help keep you on track.

One of the toughest things about adopting any new diet is dealing with lack of understanding from friends or family. Ideally encourage the whole family to follow the diet or track down blogs and forums where you can find support.

The Paleo approach is a lifestyle change. It is not about temporary fixes so it is good to take your time to help yourself adopt a new way of living that will optimize your health and promote a sense of well-being.

If you are craving carbohydrates, then try some of these Paleo alternatives:

Carb-based foods	Paleo alternative
Spaghetti, tagliatelle	Spaghetti squash, kelp noodles, spiralized courgette or carrot
Rice	Cauliflower Rice (p.115) or parsnip rice
Chips/crisps	Mashed sweet potato, cauliflower mash or root vegetable mash
Wraps made from flour e.g. wheat/corn	Lettuce 'wraps', coconut wraps, nori wraps
Tortilla crisps and other grain-based snacks	Nuts and seeds, kale crisps (p.112) dehydrated vegetable crisps, flaxseed crackers or nut and seed crackers
Couscous or quinoa	Cauliflower Rice (p.115)
Lasagne	Use strips of courgette instead of the pasta and make a dairy-free white sauce flavoured with nutritional yeast and spices
Muffins, cakes, biscuits	Make them with coconut flour or nut-based flours instead
Granola/cereals	Paleo granola made from nuts and seeds
Porridge	Chia desserts (p.139)
Energy bars/protein bars	Home-made or shop-bought alternatives made with nuts, seeds and dried fruits

Why Paleo?

The Paleo diet has been widely researched and it has been shown to have numerous health benefits. Various studies have indicated that the Paleo diet can be an effective way to lose weight, to make sure you are eating enough nutrients and to reduce the risk of many chronic diseases.

Blood Glucose Balance

As the Paleo diet avoids refined sugar and carbohydrates, it can help to improve blood glucose levels, counteract metabolic syndrome and reduce the risk of diabetes and insulin resistance.

Inflammation

Imbalances in blood sugar not only lead to weight gain and increased body fat but also promote inflammation. The Paleo diet includes plenty of anti-inflammatory nutrients, omega-3 fats and monounsaturated fats to lower the inflammatory response. A Paleo diet can therefore help to address inflammatory conditions such as asthma, arthritis and eczema.

Reduction in Allergies

The Paleo diet avoids key food groups known to be allergens, particularly gluten and dairy. By removing these foods you may find allergic reactions and associated inflammation are reduced.

Improved Digestion

The Paleo diet eliminates gluten and grains as well as other foods known to be gut irritants. The diet also includes foods beneficial for gut health and digestion, such as bone broth and fermented foods.

Body Composition

One of the benefits of the Paleo diet is a greater emphasis on high quality, protein-rich foods. These are essential for improving muscle mass and reducing body fat. Following a Paleo diet can lead to improved body composition and increased muscle mass and strength.

Cardiovascular Disease

The Paleo diet is rich in antioxidants, healthy fats and nutrients essential for a healthy heart. By avoiding sugar and processed foods including trans fats, it also eliminates ingredients known to contribute to cardiovascular disease.

Improved Energy

The Paleo diet focuses on low glycaemic foods – this means that sugars are released slowly into the bloodstream promoting sustained energy levels. By excluding refined carbohydrates and sugars, you avoid sudden highs and lows in energy that result in fatigue and a low mood.

Autoimmune Disease

Autoimmunity is a process whereby our body's own immune system attacks our cells, tissues and organs. Examples of autoimmune diseases include coeliac disease, multiple sclerosis, rheumatoid arthritis, lupus and vitiligo. Autoimmune diseases all share a common link – damage to the intestinal lining. This is sometimes referred to as 'leaky gut' or intestinal permeability. A leaky gut arises when the gut lining is damaged and some of the contents of the gut leaks into the bloodstream resulting in an immune response. This can lead to generalized inflammation and production of antibodies and auto-antibodies, which attack the cells and tissues of the body. The gut can become leaky for many reasons. It may be linked to the consumption of certain foods (gluten, grains, dairy, etc.) and lifestyle (e.g. high stress or taking medications). The Paleo diet addresses this by removing key food triggers and focuses on healing the gut to reduce the inflammatory response.

Your Daily Vitamins and Minerals

The table below shows the recommended daily amounts of some of the important vitamins and minerals needed for optimal health in the Paleo diet.

Vitamin/Mineral	Daily Requirement	Best Paleo Sources
Vitamin A	Men: 900 mcg Women: 700 mcg	Sweet potato, carrots, eggs, cantaloupe melon, butternut squash
Vitamin B_6	Men: 1.3 mg Women: 1.3 mg	Salmon, chicken, spinach, bananas, hazelnuts
Vitamin B_{12}	Men: 2.4 mcg Women: 2.4 mcg	Salmon, sardines, clams, beef, pork, chicken, eggs
Vitamin C	Men: 90 mg Women: 75 mg	Citrus fruit, strawberries, tomatoes, red peppers, broccoli
Vitamin D	Men: 15 mcg Women: 15 mcg	Salmon, sardines, eggs
Vitamin E	Men: 15 mg Women: 15 mg	Avocado, olive oil, almonds, dried apricots, papaya, spinach
Calcium	Men: 1,000 mg Women: 1,000 mg	Spinach, sea vegetables, pak choi, rhubarb, tinned sardines, almonds
Copper	Men: 900 mcg Women: 900 mcg	Raw mushrooms, cooked liver, prunes, sun-dried tomatoes
Iron	Men: 8 mg Women: 18 mg	Liver, heart, kidney, kale, spinach, mussels, clams, oysters, bone broth
Magnesium	Men: 400 mg Women: 310 mg	Cooked spinach, kale, bananas, almonds, cashews, pumpkin seeds
Potassium	Men: 2,000 mg Women: 2,000 mg	Plums, bananas, artichokes, coriander, mushrooms, almonds, walnuts
Zinc	Men: 11 mg Women: 8 mg	Beef, turkey, oysters, crab, pork, shiitake mushrooms, cashews

Why Take Supplements?

If you have been struggling with an ongoing health condition for some time, then as well as following the Paleo diet certain supplements may be helpful to you.

For many people, regardless of the diet they follow, vitamin D levels are often low. Short daily exposure (ten to 15 minutes) to the sun without sunscreen during the warmer months is enough for most people to get sufficient vitamin D. You can also get some vitamin D from foods, such as eggs and fish. However, if you live in northern latitudes where the sun is not as strong in the colder months of the year, vitamin D supplementation may be beneficial at that time. It is sensible to get your vitamin D levels tested before supplementing.

For people who do not eat much oily fish, taking a fish oil supplement daily may be a valuable addition.

Despite the benefit of taking supplements, the focus should be on getting nutrients directly from food. If you decide to take a supplement, then do so under the supervision of a healthcare practitioner. Some supplements are also not appropriate if you are taking certain medications.

If you are following the Paleo diet to support digestion and gut health, then you may benefit from including collagen and gelatine powders. There are other supplements to support gut healing and these may include glutamine, vitamin A, probiotics, colostrum and omega-3 fats. Always seek professional advice to check if supplements are appropriate for you.

The Paleo Lifestyle

The Paleo approach is not just about diet but a whole lifestyle movement. It means modelling your life after that of your ancestors in order to promote optimal health and wellness. Our genes are not just influenced by what we eat, but by how we live our lives too.

Get Moving

Most people's lives are very sedentary yet our forebears would have been moving through much of the day. They hunted, gathered, foraged and at times even migrated. Sometimes this would have been gentle exercise and at other times much more intense activity. Keeping active enables us to burn energy and support muscle mass. Gentle exercise is also a great way to unwind and reduce stress. It can also be a social experience enjoyed with other people, which in itself can be very beneficial to our health and well-being. Aim to move regularly during the day to get as much exercise as you can. In addition, include some high-intensity exercise such as sprinting. Intense bursts of activity for short periods helps to stimulate the release of growth hormone, this signals to the body to synthesize muscle tissue and can improve muscle mass and fat loss, and aerobic fitness by strengthening the heart.

Include Muscle Boosting Exercise

As we age we naturally lose muscle mass unless we deliberately exercise our muscles. Regular weight-bearing exercise is crucial for strengthening bones and supporting a healthy muscle mass. Resistance workouts, such as weight lifting, stimulate the release of anabolic hormones, particularly testosterone and growth hormone, which helps to keep you lean.

Get Quality Sleep

Sleep is essential for good health. Poor sleep can lead to blood sugar imbalances, a low mood, listlessness and a lowered immune system. It is often associated with weight gain. Sleep is vital for the release of growth hormone, which works hard during the night to repair and rejuvenate tissues. Research shows that regular, good-quality sleep is vital for emotional health, with poor sleep resulting in irritability, short-temperedness and depression. Aim for six to eight hours a night.

Socialize and Meet People

Humans are social and even spiritual beings. For optimal health and well-being it is important to spend time with friends and family who share common goals and values. If you wish to age healthily, then

focus on surrounding yourself with people who support and love you. Having a sense of community, a feeling of belonging and living with a sense of purpose are key aspects of a healthy fulfilling life.

Get Outdoors

Our ancestors spent most of their time outdoors. Regular exposure to sun provides lots of vitamin D, an essential vitamin for health and longevity that is not readily available through food. Spending time outdoors in the natural world is also a valuable way of relieving stress.

Keep an Eye on Stress

There is no easy way of escaping the day-to-day stress of modern living, but too much stress can contribute to poor health. Take steps to reduce levels of stress in your life if needed and make more time for fun, rest and relaxation.

Use Your Mind

As we age its important to ensure that we exercise our minds as well as our bodies. Keep your brain sharp with stimulating mental activities, crosswords, quizzes, reading and learning throughout your life.

Paleo Vegetarians

The Paleo focus on meat, fish and animal products means that it isn't very vegetarian-friendly. It is difficult to follow a Paleo diet if you wish to avoid all meat and fish. However, it is possible to improve a vegetarian diet following key principles of the Paleo diet.

One of the chief difficulties with a strict Paleo diet for vegetarians is that it cuts out many of the key protein sources (pulses and dairy). While nuts contain protein, they can also be inflammatory if they are eaten in excess. This is because they contain higher levels of omega-6 fats compared to omega-3. Nuts and seeds should also be soaked before using to reduce phytate levels and make them easier to digest.

Eggs are one of the best Paleo vegetarian sources of protein, and they are also rich in nutrients. Vegetarians should therefore aim to consume eggs regularly. Dairy products are not included in a strict Paleo diet, but for a vegetarian who can tolerate dairy they may be a useful addition to the diet. If you are going to include dairy then focus on grass-fed dairy products and fermented dairy. Pulses, including soy, are not consumed on the Paleo diet but vegetarians and vegans may need to add them in moderate quantities to ensure they are getting enough protein. Soaking

and sprouting beans may make them easier to digest. In addition vegans may like to include the occasional bowl of cooked quinoa or amaranth, which are reasonable sources of protein.

In view of the difficulty of obtaining enough protein, some vegetarians may feel comfortable eating a little fish and shellfish as a protein source. Vegan protein powders are available but traditionally they are based on rice, hemp, soya or pea proteins, which may not be well tolerated. Spirulina is a green algae available as a supplement that is rich in protein and it can also be a useful addition to the diet. For those with autoimmune conditions, however, it may not be appropriate as it can activate an immune response.

Non-meat eaters will also need to ensure they are getting adequate amounts of certain nutrients – in particular omega-3 fats and vitamins D and B_{12}. Another micronutrient that vegetarians and vegans might need to watch is iron. While many vegetables contain iron, it is not as readily absorbed as it is from meat sources.

It is advisable to see your doctor before adopting a Paleo vegetarian or vegan diet.

Opposite: Eggs are an excellent protein-rich, nutrient-dense Paleo food for vegetarians.

Quality Matters

The quality of the food you eat is crucial to maintain optimal health. Ideally only meat from animals raised organically on pasture and fed grass should be eaten. These animals are unlikely to have been dosed with antibiotics or hormones and the nutritional profile of their meat is generally superior. Organic is not necessarily the same as grass-fed as some farmers may include supplemental grain. From a welfare perspective grass-fed and/or organic animals are often healthier and better treated. They are less likely to be contaminated with E. coli as the contamination can come from the slaughterhouse where manure from an animal comes into contact with the meat. There is less manure on grass-fed cattle than on cattle reared indoors.

Grass-fed meats generally have a better omega-6 to omega-3 ratio and are often leaner with a higher protein content. Micronutrients and antioxidant levels are often higher. Meat and dairy products from grass-fed animals are rich in conjugated linoleic acid (CLA), which helps to support lean body composition, improve insulin sensitivity and strengthen the body's immune function.

With regards to fish, both farmed fish and fish caught in the sea or river are an excellent protein source. However, commercially farmed fish may include additives and food dyes, so if you cannot access wild fish, select organic farmed fish. Wild salmon typically contains more protein and less saturated fat than farmed fish. Both are good sources of omega-3 fats. There is also concern that farmed fish may contain more pollutants than wild-caught fish. However, as many people do not eat enough fish you are better off eating quality farm-raised salmon (without added dyes) than not eating salmon at all.

With vegetables and fruits, if possible select organically grown, local and seasonal produce. This avoids the risk of consuming pesticides. Certain produce contains more pesticide residues than others so if you cannot afford to buy all organic, then prioritize and focus on buying organic foods that are more likely to be contaminated. These include apples, celery, tomatoes, cucumber, grapes, strawberries, red peppers, potatoes, peaches and nectarines. In any case, ideally choose local produce from farmers' markets where the produce is guaranteed to be fresh.

Opposite: Wild Alaskan salmon is an excellent source of protein and essential omega-3 fats.

Paleo Autoimmune Diet

Within the framework of the Paleo diet there are many variations from which to choose. One commonly adopted is the autoimmune Paleo diet. This is valuable for anyone suffering from an autoimmune condition or chronic inflammation of the gut. The autoimmune approach removes some foods from the diet while attention is given to repairing the gut lining.

One of the principles of the Paleo diet is to avoid foods known to irritate the gut and cause intestinal permeability. This includes lectins, a class of carbohydrate-binding proteins found in many different foods including grains, pulses and pseudograins (e.g. quinoa, chia and amaranth). The consumption of lectins is associated with a number of diseases, particularly autoimmune conditions. Gluten in particular is implicated in many inflammatory and autoimmune diseases. In addition, certain food proteins, especially those found in dairy, have the ability to cross-react with gluten. This is the situation when antibodies formed against gluten by the body recognize proteins in other foods such as dairy. This means that even if gluten has been removed from the diet, the body will still mount an immune response if dairy or other cross-reactive foods are consumed. While not all people

who are sensitive to gluten will cross-react to other foods, for those with an autoimmune condition it is normally recommended that cross-reactive foods are eliminated at least initially as the gut heals.

While the majority of these problem foods are avoided in the standard Paleo diet (gluten and grains, legumes, etc.), there are some additional foods that may be aggravating for certain people. Lectins, for example, are also present in vegetables from the nightshade family – this includes tomatoes, aubergines, potatoes, chillies and peppers. Eggs are also a common allergenic food and contain lysozyme, an enzyme that may cause damage to the gut lining. While eggs are normally suitable for people on a Paleo diet, if there is damage to the gut lining it is sensible to avoid them while the gut heals. Nuts and seeds (except coconut) and sugar alcohols (such as xylitol) are also commonly excluded. Other foods that are known gut irritants, such as caffeine and alcohol, are also removed from the diet during the healing phase.

Opposite: Grilled chicken provides plenty of lean protein and makes a great salad with some leafy greens. Avoid dressing with mayonnaise as it is generally not autoimmune-friendly.

Is Dairy Paleo?

Dairy was not part of our ancestors' diet and so it is not included in the Paleo (or Paleolithic) diet. Milk and dairy products only became part of our diet about 10,000 years ago when people started to settle down and work the land in agriculture. Subsequently animals became domesticated and people began to drink milk. Milk and dairy products became part of the diet in this period, which was called the New Stone Age or Neolithic era. However, the main principle of a strict Paleo diet is to avoid all agricultural foods such as grains, pulses and dairy – like milk, cheese and yogurt.

Today dairy is prevalent in the modern Western diet and it is frequently added to many processed foods. Some people are intolerant to dairy products and research has demonstrated that milk proteins and peptides have the potential to cause allergies, inflammation, autoimmune conditions and other health problems. Many people find the proteins difficult to digest and they may irritate the gut lining and cross into the bloodstream initiating an immune response. Dairy allergy is one of the more common food allergies, particularly in children. In addition, milk is highly insulinogenic (i.e. stimulating the production of insulin), which can promote inflammation and insulin resistance. Cow's milk proteins are also known to cross-react with gluten peptides, which means that people with gluten sensitivities may also react to dairy products.

Milk and other dairy products also contain lactose, a milk sugar that must be broken down by our bodies via the enzyme lactase so that we can digest it. It is estimated that about 65 per cent of people do not have enough enzyme to digest lactose and so are lactose intolerant.

One of the concerns about eliminating dairy is how to obtain enough calcium for healthy bones. However, for optimum bone health many nutrients are required which are not provided in a good balance by eating dairy products. Key nutrients include vitamin D, calcium, magnesium, zinc, protein, collagen, boron, silicon, vitamin K and vitamin C. In fact excess calcium has also been associated with the risk of cardiovascular disease.

Some variations of the Paleo diet do include dairy products in moderation. If you wish to consume dairy, it is worth noting that there is a big difference in nutritional profile between grass-fed dairy and conventional grain-fed dairy products. Grass-fed dairy is a good source of fat-soluble vitamins and CLA, an anti-

inflammatory fat. In addition, fermented dairy products such as yogurt and kefir provide a valuable source of probiotics. Dairy, particularly butter, contains butyric acid; this is a short-chain fatty acid that can lower inflammation in our gut. Dairy fat may also help to lower blood pressure. It is filling and so may help reduce cravings and blood sugar imbalances.

If you are tolerant to dairy and wish to include it in your diet, it is best to choose whole grass-fed dairy products. Low-fat

Above: Dairy products such as milk, yogurt, butter, cream and cheese are generally excluded from a Paleo diet.

dairy is not a rich source of fat-soluble vitamins and does not appear to have the same satiating properties. If you are sensitive to lactose, then stick to low lactose dairy products such as butter or hard cheese. Home-made yogurt or kefir, which has been fermented for 12 to 24 hours, is also likely to be very low in lactose.

The Paleo Menu

Following the Paleo diet may feel daunting at first. Here are some suggestions to help you to get started.

Paleo Breakfast

Eggs are a classic breakfast meal that works well for a Paleo diet. Prepare them in different ways to add variety to your menu. Try and include a choice of vegetables alongside them. Many people following a Paleo diet will simply eat leftovers from the night before. This may mean eating a piece of meat or fish with cooked or raw vegetables.

For those who don't like a heavy breakfast, then simple no-cook options could include green smoothies, Raspberry Chia Dessert (see page 139), sliced avocado and fruit, nut cream or Home-made Coconut Yogurt (see page 187) and fruit, hard-boiled eggs and vegetable sticks. You could also make up some Paleo pancakes, Paleo bread or granola and serve it with Home-made Coconut Milk (see page 197).

If you are typically in a hurry, prepare some foods in advance that you can simply reheat. Simple meat patties made with lean minced turkey or beef can be made in advance and even frozen in batches. You can cook them and pair the dish with steamed vegetables.

Your Paleo Lunch and Dinner

Lunch and dinner options are interchangeable depending on preferences. A colourful salad with some protein is light and energizing. If you fancy a little starch add some baked sweet potato. Soups are great on cooler days, but always ensure that there is enough protein in the meal. For a less starchy substitute, try spiralized courgette and carrots or kelp noodles instead of pasta. Coconut flour wraps are also available and can be used like traditional wheat wraps.

For something more substantial, your Paleo dinner should focus on lean meats, fish or seafood cooked with spices featuring flavours that you really enjoy with a variety of vegetables.

Paleo Snacks

Snacking is not encouraged unless you are really hungry. If you do need a snack, it is best to keep it simple. This could include a handful of nuts and seeds, some fruits, vegetable sticks with nut butter, beef jerky or a smoothie. Other examples are home-made Paleo breads, tinned fish such as tuna, salmon or sardines, hard-boiled eggs, cooked meats, coconut, avocado, olives, Sauerkraut (see page 186) or Coconut Kefir (see page 185).

Example Meal Planner

Below is an example of a typical meal planner for a Paleo week. You can follow it directly or tweak it to meet your own needs. Remember to drink plenty of Paleo fluids as well.

Breakfast	Lunch	Dinner	Snacks
Omelette with vegetables	Chicken with Rocket and Orange Salad with Vinaigrette Dressing (p.156)	Spiced Venison Burgers (p.56) with vegetables; Creamy Coconut Chocolate Mousse (p.180)	Sauerkraut (p.188); Matcha Green Smoothie (p.198)
Raspberry Chia Dessert (p.139)	Salmon and Seafood Salad with Gremolata (p.98)	Hoisin Spiced Ribs (p.44), sweet potato wedges, vegetables	Chocolate Chip Banana Bread (p.160); Berry Ice Cream (p.144)
Pan-fried Indian Spiced Liver (p.62)	Tom Yum Soup with Dulse (p.130), mixed salad	Buffalo Steak (p.52), steamed vegetables; Apricot Peach Crisp (p.151)	Handful of berries with home-made yogurt, nuts and seeds
Harissa Baked Eggs with Spinach (p.88)	Mediterranean Chilli and Herb Prawns (p.104), large mixed salad	Sticky Chicken (p.70), sweet potato and vegetables; Paleo Pumpkin Tart (p.126)	Tangy 'Cheese' Kale Crisps (p.112); Coconut Kefir (p.185)
Spiced Venison Burgers (p.56) with Beetroot, Carrot and Pear Coleslaw (p.122)	Crispy Quail with Fig and Beetroot Salad and pomegranate dressing (p.82)	Almond Turkey and Green Bean Curry (p.74); Cauliflower Rice (p.115)	Berry Ice Cream (p.144), handful of nuts
Asparagus and Poached Egg with Hollandaise Sauce (p.91)	Seared Raspberry Duck with Berry Honey Dressing (p.78)	Balsamic Lamb Chops with Mint and Parsley Dressing (p.48), mixed salad	Chocolate Chip Banana Bread (p.160); Coconut Yogurt (p.187)

10 Key Principles

1 Focus on Quality
The Paleo approach is not about eating particular amounts or counting calories, but focuses on nutritional density. One of the best ways of ensuring quality is to start eating grass-fed and pasture-raised meat, wild-caught fish and organic, locally grown, seasonal fruit and vegetables.

2 Ensure Enough Protein
Many people do not consume enough protein for their body's needs, especially if they need to recover from injury. Ensure that each meal includes some protein – a palm-sized portion is enough for most people, others may need more depending if they are in training or recovering from an injury. It may seem strange to eat meat or fish at breakfast, but it doesn't take long before it becomes second nature.

3 Don't be Afraid of Fats
If you have previously followed a low-fat diet, it may seem strange to be recommending animal and saturated fats. However, these are essential for your health and are a useful energy source for your body. Switch to high quality saturated fats for cooking and eliminate all processed vegetable oils.

4 Get Variety
Look through this book to get an idea of the vast range of foods that can be included in the Paleo diet. Each week aim to include a new food – by consuming a greater variety of foods you will get a diverse range of nutrients and antioxidants in your diet that are beneficial to health.

5 Cook From Scratch
The easiest way to follow a diet is to choose a recipe and start cooking! Cooking for yourself will eliminate additives, sugars and processed oils found in commercially prepared foods and ready meals. Use the recipes in this book to get you started. You can also double recipes and then freeze in batches to help save time later.

6 Limit Sugars
While honey and other sweeteners are included in the Paleo diet, they should only be used in moderation. Sugar is inflammatory and promotes oxidative damage, which is the precursor to chronic diseases. It also leads to weight gain and an increase in body fat rather than muscle. If you suffer with blood sugar imbalances, then you may also wish to limit your intake of fruit to one or two portions a day and avoid dried fruits.

7 Include Fermented Foods

Foods containing healthy bacteria (known as probiotic-rich foods) are essential for our digestive health and overall well-being. One of the best ways to increase the levels of healthy microbes in your gut is to eat fermented foods daily. These include home-made yogurt, kefir, sauerkraut, kimchi, kombucha and pickled vegetables.

8 Keep Hydrated

Don't overlook the importance of fluids in your diet. Water is essential for digesting and absorbing foods, transporting nutrients around the body, keeping cells functioning properly and removing toxins via the liver and kidneys. If you do not drink enough water, you may feel tired and toxins can build up in your body. Ideally, choose filtered water, as it's free from potential contaminants, and either drink it plain or in broths and herbal teas. Aim for eight glasses a day. Eating fresh fruits and vegetables, soups and smoothies will also contribute to your fluid intake.

9 Construct a Balanced Plate

The easiest way to ensure that your diet is balanced is to look at what you put on your plate. Each meal should include high quality protein (at least a quarter of your plate); roughly half of your plate should be low-starch vegetables, including dark green leafy vegetables, but aim for lots of colour and variety. On the remaining quarter, you can add some starchy vegetables like butternut squash, sweet potato, carrots or beetroot. Always include healthy fats – these may occur naturally in meat or fish, or avocado and olives for example, or you may drizzle over a dressing or sauté the food lightly in fat.

10 Eat Mindfully

Take your time over meals. Rather than eating on the run, sit at a table and eat slowly and mindfully. Doing so will promote healthy digestion, slow down the release of glucose into the bloodstream keeping blood sugars more stable and will make you less likely to overeat. Listen to your body and only eat if you are truly hungry. Many people following a Paleo diet enjoy intermittent fasting while others find that their high activity levels mean they require regular meals and snacks.

Health Benefits of Paleo Meat

 Eye health: Grass-fed beef contains significant amounts of beta-carotene, which is converted by the body into retinol. This nutrient is particularly important for maintaining healthy eyesight as we age.

Heart health: Paleo meats are a good source of CLA, a fatty acid with numerous health benefits including reducing inflammation in the body, cutting body fat and lowering the risk of heart attack. Grass-fed meats also contain a higher level of omega-3 fatty acids, which are known to benefit the health of the heart.

Immune system: Grass-fed meats are a rich source of protein (needed for the production of white blood cells) as well as minerals, selenium, zinc, antioxidants, vitamin E and beta-carotene, which all help to promote a healthy immune system.

 Pregnancy health: Paleo meats are rich in essential nutrients that help to ensure a healthy pregnancy, including B vitamins (B_{12}, folate, B_6) for production of healthy red blood cells, protein for growth and development of the foetus, and choline and omega-3 fats for brain health.

 Growth and development: Grass-fed meats supply valuable nutrients that aid growth and development in children and teenagers, including B vitamins, iron and zinc that are often lacking from children's diets.

Grass-fed Beef

Grass-fed beef comes from cows that have grazed in pasture year-round rather than being fed a processed grain-based diet for much of their lives. Grass feeding improves the quality of beef, and makes the beef richer in omega-3 fats, vitamin E, beta-carotene and CLA. Beef is also an excellent source of high quality protein, vitamins and minerals such as B vitamins, iron, selenium, magnesium, zinc and choline.

Grass-fed beef may contain more than twice the amount of beta-carotene and lutein that is present in conventionally fed beef. The cholesterol content of grass-fed beef is also lower than that in conventionally fed animals. Grass-fed beef is also two to three times higher in CLA compared to the levels found in non-grass-fed beef. CLA is derived from linoleic acid, an omega-6 fatty acid which is associated

Nutrition: Grass-fed beef is a major source of omega-3 fatty acids and is naturally leaner than grain-fed beef. **Benefits:** Has lower cholesterol than grain-fed beef and may have cancer-fighting properties.

with a range of health benefits, including immune and inflammatory system support, greater bone mass, sugar regulation and reduced body fat.

Beef is a particularly important source of a number of key nutrients that are often low in people's diets including children and teenagers – they include B_{12}, B_6, zinc and iron. Beef also provides reasonable amounts of potassium and phosphorous to help keep the heart healthy.

Roast Beef

A joint of rump, sirloin or rib of beef all make succulent roasting cuts.

- Roast beef is an excellent source of immune system-supporting minerals including selenium and zinc.
- This is a particularly rich source of iron (important for maintaining healthy red blood cells), potassium, niacin and other essential nutrients.

Steak

Choose lean cuts of steak for a high-protein, low-fat meal. This includes top sirloin, rump and eye of round steak.

- An 85-g (3-oz) portion of top sirloin steak contains no carbohydrates but has all of the essential amino acids, which makes it a complete protein. This macronutrient is important for cell rebuilding, boosting the immune system and muscle growth.

Minced Beef

Lean or extra lean minced beef is a good high-protein, low-fat option. Ideal for home-made burgers, meatloaf, meatballs and taco fillings. Serve with flavoursome sauces to keep the meat moist and tender.

- Lean minced beef is a useful source of coenzyme Q_{10}, an antioxidant that helps to prevent damage to your cell membrane proteins and DNA.

Beef Ribs

A favourite for slow cooking, beef short ribs are also a popular choice for braising, slow roasting and barbecues. Marinate the ribs to ensure they are full of flavour.

- Beef ribs are an excellent source of several important vitamins. For instance, an 85-g (3-oz) serving contains more than 80 per cent of the daily recommended intake of vitamin B_{12}.

Meatloaf

HIGH PROTEIN

Meatloaf is delicious hot or cold – the addition of tomato sauce keeps the meat beautifully moist while cooking. Serve with a leafy green salad or steamed vegetables.

Prep: 20 mins/Cook: 50 mins

Ingredients (serves 4)
1 tablespoon balsamic vinegar
60 g (2 oz) tomato paste
Pinch of cayenne pepper
Squeeze of lemon juice
Pinch of garlic powder
500 g (18 oz) minced beef
2 tablespoons coconut flour
1 onion, finely chopped
60 g (2 oz) pancetta, finely chopped
1 garlic clove, chopped
1 egg, beaten
Salt and freshly ground black pepper

Method

1 Preheat the oven to 190°C (370°F/gas mark 5). Line a 500-g (2-lb) loaf tin with double-thickness baking parchment.

2 For the tomato sauce, mix the vinegar, tomato paste, cayenne, lemon juice and garlic powder together. Add a splash of water if needed and continue to mix until the sauce is smooth.

3 Tip the remaining ingredients and half of the tomato sauce into a large bowl and season with salt and pepper. Mix thoroughly – your hands are the best implements for this job.

4 Press the mixture into the loaf tin and spread the remaining sauce over the top. Bake for 40–45 minutes until the top is golden and crunchy. If the top does not colour in the oven, pop the tin under the grill and brown for 5 minutes.

5 Cool in the tin for 5 minutes, then lift out using the baking parchment and put on a board. Slice and serve.

ENERGIZING AND BUILDS MUSCLES	
Calories (per serving)	399
Protein	30.9 g
Total fat	27.0 g
of which saturates	11.5 g
Carbohydrates	7.5 g
of which sugars	2.9 g
Vitamins/minerals	B, zinc, iron, selenium

Pastured Pork

A popular white meat packed with plenty of health-promoting nutrients. Pork is a high-protein food making it ideal for building muscle and supporting the immune system. The fat content varies depending on the cut of meat.

Pork is useful for building energy levels as it is packed with an array of vitamins

Nutrition: Pastured pork is high in omega-3 fatty acids and contains more vitamin E than grain-fed pork.
Benefits: May help to lower cholesterol, good for cardiovascular health and helps with energy levels.

and minerals. A 100-g (3½-oz) serving of pork provides 65 per cent of your RDA of thiamin, the B vitamin necessary for the efficient metabolism of carbohydrates into energy. It is also essential for the growth and repair of muscle fibres. High levels of vitamins B_2 and B_3 (riboflavin and niacin) together with minerals such as phosphorus, magnesium, iron and zinc regulate energy release throughout the day and help your immune system to fight off illness.

Pork Tenderloin

The leanest cut of pork comes from the loin. Pork tenderloin has a similar fat content to a skinless chicken breast. Marinades can stop the meat from drying out during cooking.

- Tenderloin is considered an excellent source of vitamin B_{12} and the B vitamins thiamin and niacin, all of which help to keep your heart healthy.

Pork Chops

Look for pork loin or sirloin chops for the leanest cuts, which may be grilled, baked, sautéed or braised. A good source of protein and, depending on the cut, most of the fat content is unsaturated.

- Pork chops are particularly high in selenium, important for thyroid function.
- This meat provides iron and B vitamins, important for maintaining energy levels.

Pork Belly

Pork belly is composed of layers of fat and meat that cook down into a flavoursome dish. 30 g (1 oz) of raw pork belly contains 15 g fat, a third of which is in the form of saturated fat.

- Pork belly has a lower protein content than other cuts of pork.
- This cut contains small amounts of iron, vitamin E and B vitamins.

Pork Spare Ribs

Pork spare ribs are inexpensive, full of flavour and can be grilled, roasted or slow-cooked. But they are a fattier cut of meat.

- Rich in B vitamins, pork spare ribs can assist in the metabolism of fat, protein and carbohydrates and promote cardiovascular health.
- Pork spare ribs provide a good source of zinc, iron, selenium and magnesium.

Hoisin Spiced Ribs

HIGH ENERGY

Slow cooking the pork keeps the meat moist and full of flavour. Hoisin sauce typically contains gluten and peanuts so this recipe includes a healthier Paleo option. This will make more home-made hoisin sauce than the recipe needs, so store it in the refrigerator to use in other recipes, or to drizzle over the cooked ribs when served.

Prep: 15 mins/Cook: 2 hrs 10 mins

Ingredients (makes about 16 ribs)

650 g (30 oz) pork spare ribs cut into single ribs and halved

½ teaspoon Chinese five-spice powder

1 tablespoon coconut oil

1 teaspoon grated root ginger

1 garlic clove, crushed

1 tablespoon tamari or coconut aminos

1 tablespoon sweet chilli sauce

60 g (2 oz) honey

2 tablespoons dry sherry, optional

Salt and freshly ground black pepper

Home-made hoisin sauce

4 tablespoons tamari

2 tablespoons almond nut butter

1 tablespoon honey

2 teaspoons rice wine vinegar

1 garlic clove, finely chopped

2 teaspoons sesame seed oil

1 teaspoon chilli hot sauce

Pinch of black pepper

Method

1 Make up the home-made hoisin sauce by placing all the ingredients in a food processor and processing until smooth. Store in the refrigerator until required.

2 Preheat the oven to 140°C (285°F, gas mark 1). Rub the ribs with the Chinese five-spice powder and season. Place on a roasting tray and cover with foil. Cook in the oven for 1 hour.

BOOSTS THE IMMUNE SYSTEM	
Calories (per rib)	103
Protein	7.8 g
Total fat	6.3 g
of which saturated fat	2.7 g
Carbohydrates	3.3 g
of which sugars	3.3 g
Vitamins/minerals	B, niacin, zinc, selenium

3 To make the sauce for the ribs, heat the oil in a frying pan and sauté the ginger and garlic for 1 minute. Add 2 tablespoons of the home-made hoisin sauce with the remaining ingredients and mix well. Remove the ribs from the oven and pour over the sauce. Mix well to coat them all over.

4 Cook for a further 30 minutes. Remove the foil and continue to cook for another 30 minutes until golden.

Grass-fed Lamb

Select organic, grass-fed lamb, which has a higher nutritional profile. Unfortunately, even the term 'grass-fed' is not a guarantee of quality since grass-fed lambs may have spent a relatively small amount of time feeding on grass. The standard to look for on the label is '100% grass-fed'. Lamb can only technically be called lamb for the first year of its life. In its second year it is called hogget, while in its third year, the meat is classed as mutton.

Grass-fed lamb contains an impressive amount of omega-3 and conjugated linoleic acid (CLA) which has anti-inflammatory and immune-system supportive properties. As pasture-fed lambs are more active, they also contain less fat and more protein than lambs reared indoors. Lamb contains many nutrients beneficial for heart health – the fatty acid profile with a high level of protective monounsaturated fats together with omega-3 and CLA are associated with low levels of inflammation. Grass-fed lamb is a source of the antioxidant minerals selenium and zinc, which help protect the body from oxidative stress. It is a rich source of B vitamins which help to maintain healthy levels of homocysteine. As a high-protein food it can also have a beneficial effect on blood sugar levels.

Nutrition: Grass-fed lamb is a good source of vitamin B12, protein, selenium, zinc and niacin.
Benefits: Reduces the risk of heart disease and helps with the regulation of blood sugar.

Lamb Shank

Lamb shanks are a popular cheaper cut of meat. They are best braised and slow cooked, as there is too much muscle on them to be roasted. To tenderize the meat, marinate lamb shanks before cooking.

- One 85-g (3-oz) serving of lamb shank contains 22.7 g of protein.
- Lamb shanks provide a good source of iron, zinc, potassium and selenium.

Leg of Lamb

A popular roasting joint, which can be cooked quickly or slow roasted for many hours so that the meat eventually falls off the bone.

- One 85-g (3-oz) serving contains around 24 g of protein and 7.8 g of fat.
- Leg of lamb is high in zinc, an important mineral for hormone production and maintaining fertility.

Minced Lamb

This is a convenient and tasty choice for home-made burgers, patties or chillies. For a lower fat option, look for lean or extra lean minced lamb.

- Minced lamb is a good source of niacin (vitamin B₃), which helps to boost your cognitive function and also promotes healthy skin.

Shoulder of Lamb

A popular roasting joint, lamb shoulder is generally cheaper than a leg joint and fattier – which can enhance its flavour. Lamb shoulder has a strong taste which means it works well with spices, herbs and sauces. It can also be diced or minced to use in curries, tagines and casseroles.

- Shoulder of lamb is high in iron, good for the formation of red blood cells.

Balsamic Lamb Chops with Mint and Parsley Dressing

GOOD FAT

A simple dish that works well with lamb steaks. To maximize the flavour, marinate the lamb overnight. The dressing is equally delicious served with a roasted lamb joint.

Prep: 1 hr 15 mins/Cook: 8 mins

Ingredients (serves 4)

1 tablespoon olive oil
2 tablespoons balsamic vinegar
1 teaspoon chopped rosemary
8 small lamb chops or 4 lamb steaks

Dressing

2 tablespoons finely chopped fresh mint
2 tablespoons finely chopped fresh parsley
1 teaspoon capers, chopped
1 anchovy, finely chopped
1 tablespoon honey
1 tablespoon balsamic vinegar
2 tablespoons red wine vinegar
4 tablespoons olive oil

Method

1 Combine the oil, vinegar and rosemary in a bowl. Flatten the lamb chops or steaks slightly with a rolling pin. Place in a shallow dish and cover with the oil mixture. Turn the meat over to coat them on both sides and marinate for at least 1 hour.

2 Whisk all the ingredients together for the dressing and set aside.

3 Remove the lamb from the marinade and place on a lined baking sheet. Put under the grill for 3–4 minutes on each side until cooked. Cover with foil and leave to rest for 5 minutes. Serve with salad leaves and the herb dressing.

PROMOTES A HEALTHY HEART	
Calories (per serving)	457
Protein	23.6 g
Total fat	37.9 g
of which saturated fat	12 g
Carbohydrates	4.5 g
of which sugars	4.5 g
Vitamins/minerals	B, zinc, iron, selenium

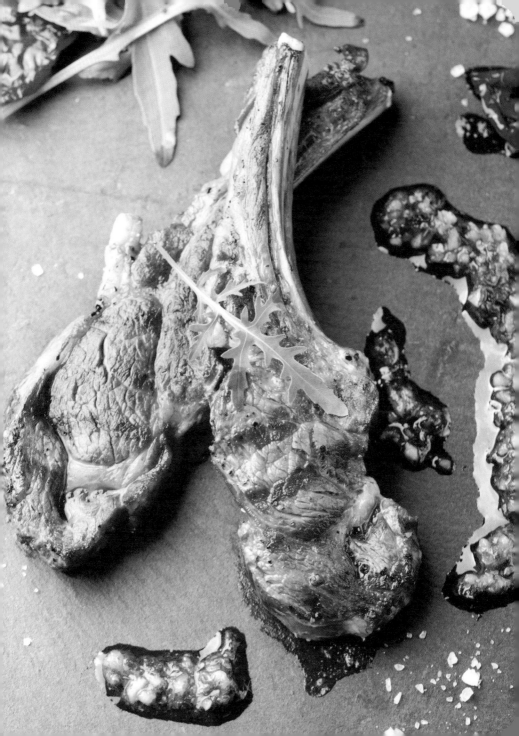

Buffalo and Bison

Buffalo and bison are different animals but the names are sometimes used interchangeably. In the United States buffalo is typically used to describe the American bison. The bison is North America's largest native animal which has been extensively farmed since the 1990s. Water buffalo originally came from Asia and are different from North American buffalo, or bison.

In parts of Europe, water buffalo are an important farm animal. They originally descended from Asian buffalo. They are called water buffalo as in the wild they inhabit swampy, wet areas. The taste of water buffalo meat and bison is very similar to beef. Water buffalo meat also contains less fat and cholesterol, and more protein, than beef and is now available in the United States.

In Europe water buffalo are also farmed to produce buffalo mozzarella and buffalo milk. Buffalo milk contains 50 per cent more protein than cow's milk, 40 per cent more energy in calories, nearly 40 per cent more calcium and high levels of the antioxidant tocopherol. It also has twice as much fat – spread evenly across saturated, mono- and polyunsaturated fats. This high fat content makes it excellent for cheese making. Some people who are allergic to or intolerant of cow's milk can tolerate buffalo

Nutrition: Buffalo and bison are excellent sources of vitamin E, iron and other essential fatty acids.
Benefits: May reduce the risk of cancer, diabetes, obesity and some immune disorders.

milk. It does contain lactose so it is unlikely to be suitable for anyone with a lactose intolerance or anyone on a strict Paleo diet.

Bison is a low-fat meat and varies in tenderness dependent on the cut. A 85-g (3-oz) serving of bison contains 16 g of protein, 190 calories and 14 g of fat. Bison is also a good source of B_{12} for a healthy nervous system. A similar serving of water buffalo contains 23 g of protein, 111 calories and 2 g of fat.

Both bison and water buffalo meat contain significant amounts of omega-3 polyunsaturated fats, which are believed to protect against heart disease and other inflammatory disorders. They are a valuable source of iron, selenium and zinc and are high in beta-carotene, an antioxidant which can reduce the risk of cancer. You can cook the meat like beef in burgers, roasts, steaks and casseroles, but as they are naturally lower in fat than beef, it is important that they are not overcooked.

Bison/Buffalo Steak

Bison or buffalo steaks come in a wide variety of cuts, like beef. They are an ideal choice for frying in a grill pan and stir-frying. Do not overcook as they require less cooking time than beef steaks.

- Grass-fed bison or buffalo steak is lower in calories, fat and cholesterol than either chicken or fish and contains nearly 70 per cent more iron than beef.

Minced Bison/Buffalo Meat

Minced bison or buffalo meat can be used in the same way as minced beef. It is generally leaner than minced beef and so will cook slightly more quickly. It is best to cook it over a low temperature to keep the meat moist.

- Minced bison or buffalo meat is a good source of B vitamins including niacin, which keeps the skin and hair healthy.

Roast Bison/Buffalo

Chuck roast, which is a less tender cut of bison or buffalo, is delicious roasted but is best marinated or pot-roasted in a liquid meat stock.

- Roast bison or buffalo meat is a good source of thiamin, which is helps to maintain a healthy nervous system.
- This meat contains zinc and selenium, which can boost the immune system.

Buffalo Steak with Mushroom Stroganoff Sauce

LOW FAT

Seared buffalo steaks drizzled with a light mushroom sauce make a delicious alternative to beef steak. Cook the steaks for just a short time to keep the meat beautifully tender and moist. You can serve sweet potato fries and salad as a tasty accompaniment.

Prep: 10 mins/Cook: 26 mins

Ingredients (serves 4)

4 buffalo steaks
Salt and freshly ground black pepper
Sprigs of oregano, to garnish

Dressing

2 tablespoons coconut oil or butter
1 onion, chopped
2 garlic cloves, chopped
500 g (18 oz) chestnut mushrooms, sliced
2 teaspoons arrowroot
1½ teaspoons smoked paprika
2 teaspoons tomato purée
400 ml (14 fl oz) beef stock
Dash of brandy, optional
4 tablespoons coconut cream
Handful of parsley, chopped

Method

1 To make the sauce, heat 1 tablespoon of the coconut oil in a frying pan and sauté the onion over a low heat for about 10 minutes until soft. Add the garlic and mushrooms, increase the heat and fry until all the liquid has evaporated. Mix the arrowroot with 1 tablespoon of water to form a paste and reserve.

2 Add the paprika and tomato purée to the mushrooms. Pour in the beef stock and brandy (if you are using it) and simmer to reduce the sauce by half. Add the arrowroot paste, coconut cream and parsley and stir for 1 minute to thicken the sauce. Season to taste.

3 Keep the sauce warm while you cook the buffalo steaks.

4 Heat the remaining coconut oil in a frying pan over a medium-high heat. Season the steaks and cook for 3 minutes on each side for medium-rare, depending on the thickness of the meat. Remove from the pan and rest covered with foil for 5 minutes. Serve the steaks with the sauce poured over, garnished with oregano.

AIDS GROWTH AND DEVELOPMENT	
Calories (per serving)	298
Protein	37.5 g
Total fat	13.1 g
of which saturated fat	9.8 g
Carbohydrates	6.7 g
of which sugars	3.4 g
Vitamins/minerals B, zinc, iron, magnesium	

Venison, Hare and Rabbit

Wild or pasture-fed venison, hare and rabbit are high quality, nutritious meats. Venison is particularly rich in protein and is an excellent source of vitamins B_6 and B_{12}. Hare and rabbit contain high levels of iron and are low in calories. They all contain lower amounts of omega-6 fatty acids and higher amounts of omega -3.

Nutrition: Venison, hare and rabbit are low in saturated fat and contain high levels of iron and selenium.
Benefits: May help to reduce risk of heart attacks, prevent anaemia and is good for keeping up energy levels.

Osso Buco

The osso buco part of the deer comes from the shank of the leg. It is considered to be a particularly flavoursome portion of meat. This part of the leg bone has a hole containing marrow in it and that allows for even cooking throughout the steak.

- Wild or pasture-fed venison is a particularly good source of omega-3 fatty acids to help protect the heart.

Venison Loin (Saddle)

Prime cuts of deer such as loin are lean cuts. To keep the meat moist during cooking you need to add a little extra fat or bacon. Try serving it with watercress salad and horseradish sauce.

- Venison contains more iron than beef, making it an ideal meat to serve growing children and teenagers, and women during pregnancy.

Roast Venison

The roast is what is taken from the rump or hindquarter of a deer. The haunch, or back leg, is popular for roasting on or off the bone, like a leg of lamb. Leftover venison meat is delicious cold and thinly sliced in salads.

- A typical serving of roasted venison contains 140 calories, less than 1 g of fat and 26 g of protein.

Hare

Known for its rich, gamey flavour, hare is a true wild meat. The brown hare is most commonly sold. It is hung to allow the flavour to develop. As the meat has a tendency to dry out, braising is the preferred cooking method. It is also popular in casseroles and stews.

- Good protein with high levels of vitamin B_3 – a key nutrient for brain health.

Rabbit

Rabbit is more delicate in flavour than hare. It is also low in fat, particularly saturated fat. It provides a range of B vitamins including B_{12} and niacin. Niacin aids the conversion of carbohydrates to energy and supports healthy cholesterol levels.

- Rabbit provides us with several useful minerals including selenium, iron and phosphorus to keep body cells healthy.

Spiced Venison Burgers

ENERGIZING

Minced venison is widely available and is perfect for making home-made burgers. To keep it moist, this recipe includes a little bacon. Serve the burgers with raw fermented pickles or sauerkraut and accompany them with salad.

Prep: 15 mins/Cook: 20 mins

Ingredients (serves 4)

1 teaspoon coconut oil, plus extra
   for frying
½ onion, diced
1 garlic clove, crushed
450 g (1 lb) minced venison
4 rashers of streaky bacon, minced
1 tablespoon chopped fresh coriander
1 teaspoon ground cumin
1 teaspoon garam masala
1 egg
Salt and freshly ground black pepper

Method

1 Heat the coconut oil in a frying pan and gently sauté the onion and garlic for about 3–4 minutes until soft. Leave to cool.

2 Place all the ingredients in a large bowl and mix them together well. Season with salt and pepper.

3 Divide the mixture into four burgers. Ensure the burgers are squeezed tightly into shape so that they will hold together when cooking.

4 Heat a little coconut oil in a large non-stick frying pan and fry the burgers. Turn them once only, cooking for about 5–6 minutes each side. Alternatively, you can cook them under a grill for the same time, turning them halfway through.

BUILDING HEALTHY MUSCLES	
Calories (per serving)	181
Protein	29.2 g
Total fat	7.0 g
of which saturated fat	2.5 g
Carbohydrates	0.7 g
of which sugars	0.4 g
Vitamins/minerals	B, magnesium, iron

Nose-to-Tail Meat

Eating every part of an animal makes good ecological sense and is a more sustainable approach to consuming meat than discarding parts of the carcass. Offal refers to the edible parts other than muscle meat. It is therefore meat including organ and other cuts such as cheek, tripe (stomach) and tongue, as well as bones (including marrow bones). Organ meat is the most nutrient-dense part of the animal. For those with inflammatory or autoimmune conditions, nose-to-tail meat provides a concentrated source of key nutrients to support gut healing.

If you don't like the taste of organ meat then try grinding some in a food processor and adding it to minced beef or lamb when you prepare some of your favourite dishes. You can also cook it and then blend it into tasty gravies, sauces and stews.

Nutrition: Nose-to-tail meat, especially liver, is rich in vitamin A, while heart is high in iron.
Benefits: Helps to keep the immune system, skin and gut healthy and helps prevent bleeding gums.

Try including organ meat weekly in your diet to support overall health, sustain energy levels and to aid healing.

Liver is one of the most popular types of organ meat and one of the most concentrated sources of vitamin A – good for maintaining a healthy immune system.

Remember that meat products from pasture-raised animals are much higher in nutrients than similar cuts that come from commercially fed livestock.

What About Toxins in Liver?

Some people worry about consuming liver as they think that the liver is a storage organ for toxins in the body, and so it may itself be high in toxins. While it is true that the liver does help to eliminate toxins, it does not actually store these substances. In fact, toxins are more likely to accumulate in the body's other fatty tissues. As with all meat, it is better to source organ meats from animals that have been raised on fresh pasture and are free of any addition of hormones, antibiotics or commercial feed additives.

Beef and Calves' Liver

Beef – and calves' – liver is stronger in flavour than some other animal livers. It is popular sautéed with onions. To tenderize liver and tone down the flavour and aroma, cut it into strips and soak in lemon juice for a few hours before draining and cooking.

- Beef liver provides a concentrated source of many key nutrients including the B vitamins (B_2, B_3, B_5, B_6, B_{12} choline and folate), which benefit some of your most important cognitive and neurological processes. Choline is important for improving the memory and it may also help to protect against fatty liver disease. The iron in liver is especially useful for people who suffer from fatigue as well as for growing children.

- Beef liver also contains CoQ10 (Coenzyme Q10), an antioxidant that helps your body to produce energy and promotes a healthy heart.

Lambs' Liver

Lambs' liver is high in protein and iron and while it also contains cholesterol, this is essential for the production of hormones in our body.

- Lamb's liver is rich in B_{12}, iron and copper – essential for the production of healthy red blood cells.

- This is a good source of vitamin A to keep eyes, skin and hair healthy.

Chicken Liver

Milder in flavour than beef or lambs' liver. Chicken liver is popular in pâtés and parfaits. Remove and discard any sinew on the chicken livers before cooking, as they will make them taste bitter if left on.

- A good source of vitamins A and C for immune health and all the B vitamins. It is a high-protein, low-calorie food rich in the antioxidants zinc and selenium.

Tongue

In general, beef and veal tongues are the most commonly consumed. They tend to have a slightly grainy, firm texture. As they can be quite chewy, they are normally stewed, boiled or poached.

- A rich source of zinc, which keeps the immune system healthy.
- Tongue provides a reasonable level of iron and B_{12} to help prevent anaemia.

Kidney

Beef, lamb and pork kidneys are generally sold trimmed, with the outer membranes removed. Beef kidneys have a milder flavour. To prepare, rinse well then soak in water with a little salt for several hours.

- A good source of B vitamins that help to maintain a healthy nervous system and metabolism.
- Kidneys contain vitamin A for vision.

Heart

Because it is a muscle meat, heart is very similar to steak or minced beef. It is often sautéed or grilled after soaking in brine for a couple of hours.

- Heart is rich in a number of nutrients including B vitamins, selenium, zinc, phosphorus and CoQ10.
- High in protein, which makes it a valuable muscle-boosting food.

Sweetbreads

Sweetbreads principally comprise the thymus and pancreas glands of a calf or young cow, lamb or pig. In general, sweetbreads are pinkish-white in colour. They have a slightly sweet taste and can be coated in ground nuts or coconut flour and sautéed in oil until crispy.

- Sweetbreads are a good high-protein food, but high in fat and cholesterol.

Tripe

Tripe is generally defined as the stomach lining of sheep, goats, pigs or deer. It has a somewhat rubbery texture and is normally boiled for at least two to three hours to make it tender. It is then usually served in stews or casseroles or used in salads.

- Tripe is rich in potassium, which is important for heart health, muscle strength and kidney function.

Pan-fried Indian Spiced Liver

PROTEIN RICH

A delicious dish that is quick to produce and which makes an energizing breakfast or light lunch option. It is nutrient-rich and anti-inflammatory thanks to the addition of the spices. Serve with some wilted spinach or a salad, if desired.

Prep: 15 mins/Cook: 10 mins

Ingredients (serves 4)

250 g (9 oz) organic chicken livers
1 tablespoon coconut oil
1 teaspoon cumin seeds
1 tablespoon grated root ginger
1 onion, finely sliced
60 g (2 oz) white mushrooms, quartered
¼ teaspoon turmeric
½ teaspoon chilli powder
½ teaspoon ground coriander
1 tomato, deseeded and chopped
Pinch of sea salt
1 tablespoon lime juice
Handful of coriander leaves, chopped

Method

1 Cut the chicken livers into cubes about 2.5 cm (1 inch) in size and reserve them. Heat the oil in a shallow pan and sauté the cumin seeds. Add the ginger and onion and cook until they are soft.

2 Add the chicken livers and sauté for 1 minute. Add the mushrooms and sauté for 2 minutes, then add the ground spices and cook for another 30 seconds. Add the tomato and season with the salt. Stir in the lime juice then remove the pan from the heat.

3 Scatter the chopped coriander leaves over the spiced liver and serve.

HAS ANTI-INFLAMMATORY PROPERTIES	
Calories (per serving)	97
Protein	12.2 g
Total fat	4.2 g
of which saturated fat	2.4 g
Carbohydrates	3.4 g
of which sugars	2.6 g
Vitamins/minerals	A, B, iron, zinc, copper

Eating Processed Meats

Cured meats (e.g. bacon, ham, salami, Parma ham and cooked sausage) have been a traditional way of preserving animal foods for hundreds of years. However, nowadays there is understandable concern not only about the quality of some of these meats, but also the presence of additives and preservatives that may increase the risk of certain cancers.

Cheap luncheon-type meats often contain less desirable cuts and animal scraps and they are often preserved with sugars, salts and nitrites. They typically also contain other fillers and additives to plump up the meat.

However, you can source naturally cured or uncured deli meats from grass-fed animals. These will be made from high-quality meat, spices, salt and sugar and be smoked. They are often cured, fermented and dried for months or even years. Although sugar is usually used in the curing process, very little remains in the finished product. Bacon, ham, sausages and other smoked meats tend to be the fattiest meats, so it is important to select grass-fed examples. The occasional addition of good-quality cured meats can be useful as a quick, convenient meal option. However, these are high in sodium which can exacerbate hypertension in salt-sensitive individuals and lead to excessive water retention. If you are concerned about nitrites, look for cured meats labelled 'nitrite free'.

When selecting cured meats, choose high-quality, grass-fed products and check the ingredients carefully. Only eat such foods occasionally – possibly as a trail food, a snack or as a topping on other dishes.

Bacon

Bacon is most commonly made from pork, although you can also find 'bacon' made from the meat of other animals like turkey. Quality bacon is an excellent source of high-protein, low-carbohydrate energy that helps to support muscle mass. Bacon

from grass-fed meats will have a healthier fat composition, supplying some omega-3 fatty acids and monounsaturated fats.

When cooking bacon, avoid making it too crispy and burnt. Burning foods can lead to the production of harmful compounds like polycyclic aromatic hydrocarbons and heterocyclic amines which are associated with cancer risk.

- A typical 100-g (3½-oz) portion of cooked bacon contains around 37 g of high-quality animal protein.
- Bacon is a good source of choline, which is necessary for memory building and cognitive function.
- It also contains a range of B vitamins to boost energy levels.

Sausages

Traditionally made from pork, sausages are now available based on a wide range of animal meats. They are a convenient meat product that can be used in a range of Paleo recipes. Not all sausages are Paleo so it is important to check the ingredients. Cheaper sausages are likely to contain fillers such as soya, refined sugar, MSG, dairy, vegetable oils or wheat starch.

Paleo-friendly sausages should consist of high-quality meat, spices, possibly some vegetables and natural animal casing. Higher quality brands will state the source of the meat used.

- A 100-g (3½-oz) pork sausage will provide around 16 g of protein.
- Pork sausages contain iron, essential for keeping muscles and tissues healthy.

Poultry and Game

Free-range and organic poultry and game are another great source of protein and they are particularly rich in an array of essential minerals including selenium, potassium, iron, magnesium, manganese and calcium, as well as plenty of B vitamins.

Proteins are the building blocks for key functions in our bodies including the production of enzymes and hormones and the maintenance of healthy bones, muscle and skin. Most adults require roughly three servings of protein-rich foods daily. Poultry and game provide a complete source of protein that is easily digested and generally low in fat. Lean meats are particularly useful for boosting energy levels as they are rich in B vitamins, which assist the body's metabolism and production of red blood cells.

It is best to choose free-range or organic poultry. Organic chicken is raised without the addition of antibiotics, synthetic hormones or pesticides and so promotes a more sustainable environment. They can roam freely and their diet contributes to healthier, cleaner meat. This means they are typically higher in protein and lower in fat than factory-farmed birds.

Health Benefits of Poultry and Game

Brain health and stress:
Poultry is high in an amino acid called tryptophan, which the body converts to the mood-boosting neurotransmitter serotonin. Serotonin can also be converted to melatonin to promote restful sleep. Poultry contains vitamin B_5 that has a calming effect on the nerves and helps to combat stress.

Heart health: Poultry is rich in B vitamins, particularly B_6 and B_{12} that help to lower the levels of homocysteine – high levels of this amino acid are linked to an increased risk of cardiovascular disease. Poultry also provides a good source of niacin (Vitamin B_3) known to decrease the LDL (low-density lipoprotein) cholesterol and triglyceride levels.

Metabolism and energy:
Poultry and game supply plenty of selenium, an essential mineral involved in metabolic function including thyroid health. They are a good source of B vitamins, which also aid metabolism and conversion of carbohydrates into energy.

Men's health: Rich in zinc and selenium, poultry has special health benefits for men by assisting in the production of testosterone. Selenium has a protective role against prostate cancer too.

Bone health: Chicken and other poultry is rich in phosphorus, an essential mineral that strengthens your teeth and bones. Its high protein content is equally important as a key nutrient for bone health and helping to prevent osteoporosis.

Chicken

A popular meat and excellent source of protein, chicken is also crammed with many essential vitamins and minerals to promote good health. For optimal benefits choose pasture-fed and/or organic chicken as this increases the omega-3 content of the meat and typically results in a leaner bird meaning more protein and less fat.

Nutrition: Chicken is very rich in B vitamins, vitamin E and the minerals selenium, zinc and niacin.
Benefits: Boosts the immune system, regulates digestion, strengthens the bones and may help with weight loss.

Chicken Breast

This is probably the most popular part of the chicken. It can be sold as a whole breast, with or without the skin, or sliced up into smaller pieces. It can be pan-fried, stuffed with herbs and spices, baked, roasted or barbecued. Use diced breast meat in stir-fries, curries or in casseroles.

▪ Chicken breast is a low-fat, high-protein option if you remove the skin.

Whole Chicken

While organic chicken may be more expensive, using the whole chicken can be a more economical option than buying individual cuts.

▪ Use the chicken bones to make a stock, which is rich in protein, minerals, like calcium for healthy strong bones, and lots of amino acids including glycine and proline to fight inflammation.

Chicken Drumsticks

These are the chicken's shins. They are cheap and easy to cook. Remove the skin to reduce the fat content of the meat.

- Being rich in darker meat, chicken drumsticks contain more myoglobin than white meat. Myoglobin is the primary oxygen-carrying protein in muscle tissue and so essential for endurance activities.

Chicken Thighs

Thighs are often considered the tastiest part of the chicken. The meat is firmer and needs longer cooking time than breast meat so are delicious roasted or in slow-cooked casseroles.

- The dark meat on chicken thighs has more fat than breast meat.
- Chicken thighs are rich in minerals such as iron and zinc and B vitamins.

Chicken Wings

These are the cheapest part of the chicken but are still fantastic to eat. They come on the bone and are typically roasted or grilled for a quick and convenient meal. Cook a batch of chicken wings and use them as a healthy protein-packed snack through the day.

- Chicken wings are rich in niacin, beneficial for healthy skin, hair and eyes.

Sticky Chicken

HIGH PROTEIN

This is a wonderful recipe for the whole family and a delicious way to use the cheaper cuts, such as thighs, drumsticks and wings. It is equally delicious with chicken breasts. Make up a big batch and use them for packed lunches or salads. You could accompany these with roasted sweet potato wedges.

Prep: 50 mins/Cook: 30 mins

Ingredients (serves 4)

450 g (1 lb) chicken drumsticks and thighs

Sticky sauce

5 tablespoons home-made low-sugar
   tomato ketchup
3 tablespoons balsamic vinegar
3 tablespoons tamari
2 tablespoons Chinese five spice powder
1 tablespoon honey
2 teaspoons olive oil
Salt and freshly ground black pepper

A GREAT IMMUNE SYSTEM BOOSTER	
Calories (per serving)	270
Protein	20.8 g
Total fat	17.0 g
of which saturated fat	4.5 g
Carbohydrates	8.3 g
of which sugars	8.3 g
Vitamins/minerals	niacin, riboflavin, zinc

Method

1 Preheat the oven to 200°C (400°F, gas mark 6). Place the chicken pieces in a large roasting tin. Whisk all the sauce ingredients together and season with salt and pepper.

2 Pour the sauce over the chicken. Toss together and make sure that the chicken is well coated and not heaped in more than one layer in the tin. Ideally marinate for 30 minutes.

3 Place the roasting tin in the oven and bake for around 30 minutes – check to see if it is done by piercing the flesh in its thickest part with a knife – it should be hot in the middle with no pinkness.

4 Serve the sticky chicken pieces hot or cold with salad and some home-made tomato ketchup, if desired.

Turkey

Turkey is a high-protein lean meat that is also packed with energizing B vitamins and iron. It is an excellent source of the amino acid tryptophan, which produces serotonin and plays an important role in strengthening the immune system and lifting mood. Turkey meat is sold in various forms, including whole, pre-packaged slices, breast, thighs, minced and fillets. If you can, buy organic. Turkeys raised organically on pasture will have been treated humanely and are less likely to contain hormones, antibiotics and traces of pesticide. Organic, pasture-raised turkey usually has higher nutrient quality. Allowed ample time to forage, the birds' meat is higher in healthy omega-3 fatty acids. Avoid buying pre-packaged slices which may be processed and full of additives and sugars. Refrigerated raw turkey can keep

Nutrition: Turkey is packed with B vitamins, potassium, iron, zinc, niacin and phosphorus.
Benefits: Boosts the immune system, helps with proper functioning of the thyroid and helps to lower cholesterol.

for one or two days, while cooked turkey will keep for about three to four days. Be careful when handling raw turkey and ensure that it does not come in contact with other food, particularly any that will be served uncooked.

The most popular way to serve turkey is as a roast. The bird comprises white breast meat and dark leg meat. Any leftovers can be used for other dishes and the bones can be boiled to make a nourishing stock.

Turkey Breast

A high-protein lean option. Just 110 g (4 oz) of skinned breast will provide 30–35 g of protein, with less than 1 g of total fat.

- Turkey breast is high in protein so can help keep post-meal insulin levels in a healthy range, encourage muscle mass and aid weight loss.
- This meat is rich in niacin to help the release of energy from foods.

Turkey Thigh

Thigh joints are delicious stuffed and roasted and ideal for feeding two to three people.

- Turkey thigh contains more iron than breast meat, which helps anaemia.
- Turkey contains the amino acid tryptophan, which produces serotinin that helps to keep the immune system healthy and promotes sleep.

Turkey Leg

A typical serving of turkey leg contains slightly less protein than breast does.

- Turkey leg is high in health-promoting minerals, such as zinc and iron.
- This meat is also a good source of selenium, a mineral needed to protect cells in the body from damage and to support the immune system.

Minced Turkey

Minced breast and thigh is readily available. Use in exactly the same way as other kinds of minced meat – slow-cooked chilli, burgers and meatballs are all easy and flavoursome options.

- Minced thigh meat tends to have a higher fat content than minced turkey breast, but it also has a deeper flavour.

Almond Turkey and Green Bean Curry

BRAIN BOOSTING

A rich-tasting creamy curry packed with anti-inflammatory ingredients useful for stimulating immune system health. This warming dish is an ideal way to use up leftover cooked turkey as well. Simply add the cooked turkey meat at the end of cooking. This dish can be prepared ahead of time and reheated when needed. Serve with Cauliflower Rice (see page 115) and a leafy green salad.

Prep: 2 hrs 20 mins/Cook: 30 mins

Ingredients (serves 4)

450 g (1 lb) turkey meat, cut into cubes
2 teaspoons olive oil
¼ teaspoon sea salt
2 teaspoons turmeric
1 tablespoon coconut oil
1 red onion, diced
300 g (10 oz) green beans, halved
4 tomatoes, chopped
1 x 400 g (14 oz) can whole coconut milk
6 kaffir lime leaves, finely shredded

Juice and grated zest of 1 lime
1 tablespoon coconut sugar or xylitol
30 g (1 oz) flaked almonds, toasted
Few coriander leaves, chopped
Strips of root ginger

Spice paste

1 onion, chopped
2 teaspoons fresh root ginger, grated
4 garlic cloves, peeled
2 teaspoons ground cumin
1 teaspoon turmeric
1 teaspoon ground coriander
1 red chilli, deseeded and chopped
60 g (2 oz) blanched almonds
1 tablespoon tomato purée

ANTI-INFLAMMATORY	
Calories (per serving)	420
Protein	42.5 g
Total fat	21.4 g
of which saturated fat	5.5 g
Carbohydrates	16 g
of which sugars	10.5 g
Vitamins/minerals	C, phosphorous, iron

Method

1 Place the turkey meat in a dish and rub over the olive oil, salt and turmeric. Marinate the turkey for a couple of hours, or overnight if possible.

2 Put all the ingredients for the spice paste in a liquidizer and process to form a thick paste. Add a splash of water if needed to create a smooth mixture.

3 Heat a large frying pan over a high heat, add the coconut oil and fry the turkey meat for 4–6 minutes, or until golden brown on all sides. Remove the turkey from the pan.

4 Add the onion and the spice paste to the pan and stir-fry for 2–3 minutes, or until fragrant. Add the green beans, tomatoes and turkey and cook for 5–6 minutes. Add the coconut milk, lime leaves, lime juice, zest and sugar. Simmer, uncovered, for a further 10 minutes, or until the turkey is tender and cooked through.

5 Scatter over the toasted flaked almonds, chopped coriander and strips of root ginger to serve.

Duck

Often dismissed as a fatty meat, duck is a good source of high-quality protein and with the skin removed it is actually low in fat and calories. Rich and full of flavour, duck meat is extremely nutritious, with high levels of B vitamins, vitamins C and A and minerals such as zinc, potassium, selenium, magnesium and iron.

Nutrition: Duck is a good source of protein and contains riboflavin, folate, thiamin and niacin.
Benefits: Improves the immune system, helps keep the skin healthy and encourages hair growth.

Duck Breast

A popular choice which, without the skin, is a lean, high protein meat. Marinate duck breasts to add extra flavour and moisture. Slash the skin a couple of times to help the marinade penetrate further. Often pan-fried, grilled or roasted.

- Duck breast is a useful source of selenium – an essential immune-supporting mineral.

Duck Thighs/Legs

Duck thigh and leg meat is slightly fattier than breast meat. Duck is a good source of iron, which plays a crucial role in the production of healthy red blood cells. This makes duck a good choice for growing children and teenagers. Use in stews.

- Duck thighs contain iron, which regulates numerous metabolic activities and plays an important role in growth.

Why Eat Ostrich?

Ostrich meat is becoming a popular healthy option and for good reason. Lower in calories and fat than chicken, it is an excellent source of protein and creatine, both important for building muscle. Ostrich is sold in the form of steaks, fillets, burgers, sausages, roasts and minced meat, and it provides plenty of energizing iron and B vitamins. Ostrich meat is similar to beef in taste and texture making it an ideal lean alternative to red meat.

As it is a lean meat, ostrich steak cooks faster than some other white meats and is usually barbecued, grilled, pan-fried, roasted or braised. Marinate or drizzle the ostrich meat with a little olive oil to keep the flesh moist when cooking. As it is high in protein and low in fat, it is a useful choice if you want to lose weight.

Below: Ostrich steak is delicious pan-fried with pepper and spices.

Seared Raspberry Duck with Berry Honey Dressing

ENERGIZING

An easy-to-make dish, which is sweet and tangy thanks to the addition of raspberry vinegar and honey. If time allows, marinate the duck breasts for a couple of hours before cooking. The dressing is equally delicious drizzled over steamed vegetables or salad.

Prep: 2 hrs 20 mins/Cook: 25 mins

Ingredients (serves 4)
4 duck breasts
1 red onion, diced
Salt and freshly ground black pepper

Marinade
4 tablespoons tamari
1½ tablespoons honey
4 tablespoons raspberry vinegar
2 tablespoons olive oil

Dressing
4 tablespoons raspberry vinegar
2 tablespoons balsamic vinegar
2 tablespoons olive oil
3 tablespoons walnut oil
½ teaspoon Dijon mustard

Method

1 Whisk all the ingredients for the dressing together, season and reserve.

2 Score the skin on the duck breasts with a sharp knife and season with salt and pepper. Combine all the ingredients for the marinade and season. Place the duck in a shallow ceramic dish and pour over the marinade. Toss to coat, cover and leave to marinate for 1–2 hours.

3 Heat a non-stick sauté pan until hot. Drain the duck breasts, discarding the marinade, and sear the breasts with the skin side down. Reduce the heat to medium and cook for 10 minutes until the fat has rendered.

4 Preheat the oven to 200°C (400°F, gas mark 6). Transfer the duck breasts to a roasting tin and cook in the hot oven for 10 minutes.

5 Remove from the oven and leave to rest for 10 minutes. Slice thinly and arrange on a plate.

6 Sauté the onion in the sauté pan with the duck fat for 1–2 minutes until softened. Sprinkle the onion over the duck breasts and drizzle over the dressing.

7 Serve with steamed vegetables or mixed salad.

BOOSTS THE IMMUNE SYSTEM	
Calories (per serving)	449
Protein	25.5 g
Total fat	34.4 g
of which saturated fat	5.7 g
Carbohydrates	7.8 g
of which sugars	7.5 g
Vitamins/minerals	B, copper, selenium

Wild Game

Game birds are wild and free range in their natural habitats so if you are looking for something low in fat and high in protein, game is a delicious and healthy alternative to other red meats. They have a lower content of pro-inflammatory omega-6 fats and a higher content of anti-inflammatory omega-3 fats than other red meats.

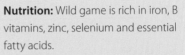

Nutrition: Wild game is rich in iron, B vitamins, zinc, selenium and essential fatty acids.
Benefits: Boosts energy levels, helps support the immune system and reduces the risk of heart attacks.

Pheasant

For maximum flavour pheasant should be hung for three days before plucking.

- Pheasant contains high levels of magnesium that is essential for stress management.
- Pheasant is rich in vitamin B_6 which plays a crucial role in the synthesis of neurotransmitters such as dopamine and serotonin, helping to boost mood.

Grouse

Grouse is the darkest of game bird meats with a rich red, almost maroon flesh, and has an intensely deep flavour to match. Red grouse is the most commonly eaten variety. As these are wild birds, they are low in fat and high in protein.

- Grouse is an excellent source of iron, important for the production of red blood cells and can help with fatigue.

Quail

Quail is a sweet and delicate white game meat that is low in fat and high in protein. Quail is generally farmed so check its provenance to make sure that it has not been intensively reared.

- Quail meat is a great source of copper, vitamin C, iron and various B vitamins, which are all important for generating and sustaining energy.

Partridge

Partridge is more mild in flavour than other game birds and is incredibly tender.

- Partridge is packed with iron, which helps your body's uptake of oxygen and energy production.
- This meat provides the trace element selenium, which has been linked to reducing feelings of depression and also boosts the immune system.

Pigeon

Wood pigeon is a small game bird and a good source of sustainable meat. High in satisfying protein, it helps your body to repair and renew cells. Gamey pigeon works well with roasted root vegetables and is delicious in pies and casseroles.

- Pigeon is a particularly good source of iron, zinc and selenium to encourage a healthy immune system.

Crispy Quail with Fig and Beetroot Salad

A delicious dish inspired by the cuisine of the Middle East, and sweet and tangy thanks to the addition of pomegranate molasses. The dressing can be prepared in advance and is a fabulous addition to any salad. This recipe would also work well with other game birds.

Prep: 2 hrs 20 mins/Cook: 35 mins

Ingredients (serves 4)

4 tablespoons pomegranate molasses
1 tablespoon ground cinnamon
2 garlic cloves, crushed
8 small boneless quail
Large handful of green salad leaves
2 cooked beetroots, sliced
2 figs, quartered
1 tablespoon pine nuts
Seeds of 1 pomegranate
Salt and freshly ground black pepper

Pomegranate Dressing

5 tablespoons pomegranate molasses
Juice of ½ lemon
1 garlic clove, crushed
Pinch of ground cumin
1 teaspoon honey
4 tablespoons olive oil

Method

1 Combine the pomegranate molasses, cinnamon and garlic and rub the mixture over the quail. Ideally marinate for 1–2 hours, or overnight.

2 Make the dressing by mixing all the ingredients together, then season and reserve.

3 Preheat the oven to 200°C (400°F, gas mark 6). Place the quail in a roasting tin and cover with aluminium foil. Roast in the oven for 25 minutes.

HELPS TO BOOST MALE FERTILITY	
Calories (per serving)	410
Protein	41.8 g
Total fat	19.8 g
of which saturated fat	3.5 g
Carbohydrates	33 g
of which sugars	26.1 g
Vitamins/minerals	C, D, zinc, selenium

4 Remove the foil and cook for 10 more minutes, or until the quail are completely cooked through. Remove from the oven and leave to rest for 5 minutes.

5 Place the salad leaves in a dish with the beetroot, figs and pine nuts. Sit the quail on top and sprinkle over the pomegranate seeds. Drizzle over the dressing just before serving.

Eggs

Eggs are one of the healthiest foods you can eat. In fact, whole eggs are among the most nutritious foods in the world, as they contain a little bit of virtually every nutrient we need. Choose omega-3 enriched or pastured eggs as they are even healthier.

Eggs contain high quality proteins, fats, vitamins and minerals and are particularly rich in two amino acids – tryptophan and tyrosine – that are known to help boost our mood. While egg yolks are relatively high in cholesterol, numerous studies have confirmed that for most people eating eggs will have a minimal effect on raising cholesterol levels.

Egg yolks are also a rich source of the antioxidants lutein and zeaxanthin, which are types of carotenoids. These have powerful preventive effects for age-related macular degeneration of the eyes.

Free-range or organic eggs are far superior to caged grain-fed eggs when it comes to nutrient content. They have a higher omega-3 content and are good sources of antioxidants, vitamins A and E and beta-carotene. Eggs are also rich in brain fats like phosphatidylcholine, which the body converts to acetylcholine, a neurotransmitter that acts on our nervous system.

Egg allergy is quite common, affecting on average two per cent of the population, particularly children – although they often outgrow it. There are also concerns that eggs may cause damage to the gut lining and stimulate the immune system. For this reason people with an autoimmune condition may find it beneficial to avoid eggs initially while they heal the gut lining and lower levels of inflammation.

Health Benefits of Eggs

 Brain health: Free-range and organic eggs supply brain-boosting omega-3 fats. Two eggs provide nearly half your daily requirements for choline. Choline is a key component of acetylcholine, a neurotransmitter that carries messages between nerves and muscles and enhances memory capacity.

 Eye health: Eggs are rich in vitamin A and the carotenoids lutein and zeaxanthin that are known to be important for protecting your eyes from age-related damage. Vitamin A is also important in night vision. If you're deficient in vitamin A, your body may be producing less rhodopsin, the visual pigment enabling us to see in low-light levels.

 Muscle health: Eggs are a useful muscle-boosting food. Easy to digest, the amino acids in eggs are converted into muscle, skin, collagen and other body tissue very efficiently. One egg contains 6 g of complete protein. This is a useful food post-workout to aid muscle recovery and repair.

 Weight loss: Eggs are a high-protein satisfying food that help you feel fuller for longer and prevent cravings between meals. Eating eggs regularly can aid weight loss and boost energy levels.

Bone health: Eggs are one of the few food sources of vitamin D. Vitamin D is an essential substance required for the absorption of calcium and maintenance of healthy bones. Eggs also supply sulphur, which aids the production of collagen, important for the formation of bone and connective tissue.

Hens' Eggs

Choose organic or pastured, free-range eggs, which provide a useful source of healthy omega-3 fats.

- Eggs deliver B vitamins for energy production and plenty of B_{12} and folate to help maintain healthy levels of homocysteine. Too much homocysteine is linked to higher risk of cardiovascular disease and cognitive decline.

Quail Eggs

Quail eggs are little eggs with a slightly richer taste than hens' eggs. You can use them in baking – usually five to six quail eggs will replace one chicken egg.

- Quail eggs are very nutrient-dense and particularly rich in B_1 thiamin, which is important for a healthy nervous system.
- Quail eggs provide more iron and potassium than hens' eggs.

Duck Eggs

Duck eggs taste almost identical to chicken eggs and are roughly the same size, so you can substitute them in your recipes very easily. However, they are very high in cholesterol so they should be only eaten in moderation.

- Duck eggs are higher in protein, calcium, iron, potassium and pretty much every other major mineral than hens' eggs.

Eggs and the Autoimmune Paleo Diet

Eggs are an important part of the Paleo diet, but be aware that they may aggravate the symptoms of people with autoimmune conditions. One of the main functions of the egg white is to protect the yolk from microbial damage through the presence of enzymes, particularly lysozyme. Lysozyme can form complexes with other proteins, which can be resistant to digestion. These can cross through the gut barrier initiating an immune response that causes inflammation and damage to the gut lining. These proteins therefore damage the integrity of the gut lining leading to increased intestinal permeability. Lysozyme appears to be the most significant enzyme that causes cell membrane damage. As intestinal permeability is one of the factors linked to the initiation of autoimmune diseases, anyone with an autoimmune disease may find they benefit from avoiding eggs while they allow the gut lining to heal.

Eggs are unlikely to be an issue for people with a healthy gut lining (as long as they are not one of the relatively small number of people who suffer from an egg allergy). They make a nutritious addition to a Paleo diet.

Harissa Baked Eggs with Spinach

BRAIN BOOSTING

A delicious breakfast or lunch dish. You can cook the vegetables in advance to save time – then just crack in the eggs and bake when ready to eat. This recipe allows for one egg per person, but for additional protein it is fine to add an extra egg.

Prep: 15 mins/Cook: 20 mins

Ingredients (serves 4)

1 tablespoon coconut oil
1 red onion, finely chopped
2 red peppers, cut into chunks
2 yellow peppers, cut into chunks
2 garlic cloves, crushed
1 teaspoon harissa paste, or to taste
Pinch of smoked paprika
1 x 400 g (14 oz) tin chopped tomatoes
100 g (3½ oz) baby spinach leaves
1 tablespoon chopped fresh parsley
4 eggs
Freshly ground black pepper

Method

1 Preheat the oven to 160°C (320°F, gas mark 3). Warm the coconut oil in a frying pan and add the onion, peppers, garlic and spices. Cook slowly for 10 minutes until the peppers are soft.

2 Add the tinned tomatoes and simmer the mixture for 1–2 minutes, or until the sauce has thickened. Stir in the spinach leaves and parsley.

3 Spoon the mixture into a baking dish or individual ramekins. Make four dips into the vegetable mixture and break in the eggs. Season with pepper.

4 Bake in the oven for 6–8 minutes until the whites are fully set but the yolks are still creamy.

PROMOTES HEALTHY EYES AND BONES	
Calories (per serving)	156
Protein	9.4 g
Total fat	8.5 g
of which saturated fat	3.6 g
Carbohydrates	10.4 g
of which sugars	9.1 g
Vitamins/minerals	D, B, C, K, A, calcium

Cooking Eggs

Eggs are a convenient, inexpensive, nutrient-dense, protein-packed food and are incredibly versatile. Here are some of the healthier ways to cook them.

Poached

The antioxidant properties in eggs are greatly reduced during cooking, particularly when eggs are fried or microwaved. Poaching eggs is one of the

healthiest options as it retains more of the valuable nutrients. As well as poaching eggs in water, you can crack eggs into a baking dish with vegetables and bake them briefly in the oven. Avoid cooking at excessively high temperatures which may damage the eggs.

Soft Boiled

When you soft boil an egg, the yolk isn't exposed to a high heat. This protects the cholesterol in the eggs from being oxidized, which could be harmful to health.

Scrambled

If you do wish to scramble eggs then use a heat-stable saturated fat such as coconut oil and cook over a low heat for as short a time as possible. Scrambling eggs can promote oxidation of the cholesterol in the egg yolk and reduce significantly the antioxidant content of the eggs.

Can I Eat Raw Eggs?

Eggs are a common allergen food and cooking eggs may change the protein structure increasing its allergenic property. For this reason some people prefer to consume raw eggs. However, eating raw eggs raises the risk of salmonella. This is more of a concern with caged birds which are intensively reared in unhygienic conditions. Free-range birds raised in

clean, spacious environments are less likely to be contaminated. Raw egg whites contain a glycoprotein called avidin that is very effective at binding biotin, one of the B vitamins. Thus consumption of egg whites on their own could lead to a biotin deficiency. As egg yolks are very rich in biotin, it is unlikely that consuming raw whole eggs will cause a problem but if this concerns you, just eat the raw yolk.

Asparagus and Poached Egg with Hollandaise Sauce

LOW CARB

Prep: 15 mins/Cook: 15 mins

Ingredients (serves 4)

16 asparagus spears, woody ends trimmed
1 tablespoon olive oil
1 tablespoon white wine vinegar
4 free-range organic eggs
Salt and freshly ground black pepper

Hollandaise Sauce

2 teaspoons freshly squeezed lemon juice
2 teaspoons white wine vinegar
2 free-range organic egg yolks
125 g (4½ oz) coconut oil, melted
Pinch of cayenne pepper
Sea salt and freshly ground black pepper

Method

1 For the hollandaise, heat the lemon juice and vinegar in a small pan until just boiling. Cool slightly. Place the egg yolks and a pinch of salt into a food processor. With the motor running, gradually add the vinegar mixture to the egg yolks in a thin stream, until incorporated. Gradually pour in the melted coconut oil until combined and thick. If too thick, add a splash of hot water. Season with salt, pepper and cayenne.

2 Bring a pan of salted water to the boil, add the asparagus spears and cook for 1–2 minutes. Drain, place in a bowl and toss with the olive oil. Season to taste.

3 Heat a pan of water to a gentle simmer then add the vinegar. Carefully crack 2 eggs into the water. Poach for 2–3 minutes, or until the eggs are cooked to your liking, then leave to drain on kitchen paper. Repeat with the remaining 2 eggs.

4 Divide the asparagus spears equally among four serving plates. Place one poached egg on top of each serving of asparagus. Drizzle over the hollandaise sauce and serve.

GREAT SOURCE OF CALCIUM	
Calories (per serving)	406
Protein	7.7 g
Total fat	41 g
of which saturated fat	29.7 g
Carbohydrates	0.1 g
of which sugars	0.1 g
Vitamins/minerals	D, E, C, B, iron, zinc

Fish and Seafood

Fish, particularly oily fish and seafood are very nutrient dense and are your best dietary source of essential omega-3 fatty acids known as EPA and DHA. They provide proteins which are also highly digestible making them an important part of your diet.

For a healthy Paleo diet, it is extremely important to include seafood in your food choices. The amino acids found in fish are easy to digest and readily bioavailable which is important for anyone with digestive issues. As they are the richest sources of long-chain omega-3 fatty acids, they can be helpful if you suffer with inflammation or autoimmune conditions.

Fish is also generally cheaper than grass-fed meat making it a cost-effective choice. Fish contains a wide range of minerals and vitamins including calcium, phosphorous, zinc, magnesium, iron and fat-soluble vitamins A, D, E, K and B_{12}. It also provides two essential minerals which are often lacking in people's diets – selenium and iodine.

The fresh fish that is available will vary according to your location and the season, but aim to include a wide variety in order to provide an array of essential nutrients. Tinned fish can also be a useful storecupboard ingredient – try and select fish in BPA-free cans where possible. BPA (bisphenol A) is an industrial chemical that is used to make resins which often line the insides of metal tins. Research in recent years has revealed the possible adverse health effects of BPA on the brains, behaviour and prostate glands of foetuses, infants and children.

Left: A selection of delicious fish and seafood.

Health Benefits of Fish and Seafood

 Thyroid function and metabolism: Seafood provides iodine and selenium which are often lacking in people's diet. Iodine is critical to healthy thyroid function. Inadequate levels of iodine causes weight gain, low energy, depression, cognitive decline and has been linked to certain cancers.

 Heart health: Oily fish provides the omega-3 fats EPA and DHA known for their heart-protective and anti-inflammatory benefits. Regular consumption of omega-3 fats has been shown to reduce the risk of heart attacks and strokes. Seafood also provides vitamins B_6 and B_{12} which can lower levels of homocysteine – a key marker for heart disease.

 Immune health: Seafood is a useful source of antioxidants including vitamin E, selenium and zinc that are important for maintaining a healthy immune system. Adequate dietary selenium has been shown to help prevent certain cancers including prostate and colorectal cancer.

Men's health: Seafood is a rich source of zinc which supports reproductive and sexual function – especially in men. They are high-protein foods and the zinc in seafood is also important for building muscle by stimulating the production of testosterone and growth hormone.

 Bone health: Seafood, particularly oily fish, is one of the best dietary sources of fat-soluble vitamin D, as well as calcium and magnesium, all essential nutrients for strong healthy bones.

Fish

Eating fish is generally beneficial for health. Fish contains omega-3 fatty acids, which can improve blood circulation, protect the heart from disease, lower cholesterol in the blood and make the skin glow. Fish also contains retinol, a form of vitamin A, which boosts night vision, and iodine, necessary for the proper functioning of the thyroid.

Nutrition: Fish is high in protein, vitamins, minerals, omega-3 fatty acids and low in calories.

Benefits: Helps with memory and keeps the brain healthy, skin firm and flexible and lowers blood pressure.

Wild Salmon

There are a number of species of Pacific salmon which are all healthy choices. These include king or chinook, sockeye, coho, pink and chum.

- This fish is especially rich in brain- and heart-healthy omega-3 fats.
- Salmon provides plenty of vitamin D needed for healthy bones and a robust immune system.

Mackerel

This protein-rich oily fish provides plenty of omega-3 fats and fat-soluble vitamins A, D, E and K to keep bones and eyes healthy.

- Mackerel contains calcium, iron, magnesium, potassium and selenium, important for keeping the heart healthy.
- Mackerel contains the antioxidant Coenzyme Q10 which helps to protect cells from damage.

Sardines

Available fresh and tinned, sardines are an oily fish rich in omega-3 fatty acids.

- Sardines are a good source of vitamin D and calcium to maintain healthy bones.
- Tinned sardines with their bones, which can be eaten, are high in calcium.
- Sardines contain energizing minerals like iron, copper and magnesium plus immune-supporting selenium and zinc.

Albacore

Albacore is a smallish species of tuna and is commonly available tinned, labelled as white meat tuna.

- Albacore is rich in protein, selenium and vitamin B_{12} and is a good source of heart-healthy omega-3 fatty acids.
- This fish is higher in mercury, so pregnant women and children should limit the amount they eat.

Tuna

Tinned tuna is inexpensive and is packed with protein.

- Tinned tuna is rich in niacin, a B-vitamin that supports healthy skin and the nervous system.
- Tuna provides B_{12} which aids the formation of red blood cells.
- Fresh tuna supplies more omega-3 fatty acids than tinned.

Sea Bass

Both sea and freshwater bass are a low-calorie, high-protein food rich in selenium and essential omega-3 fatty acids. Buy line-caught sea bass if possible.

- Sea bass is a good source of vitamin A, important for the immune system and a healthy skin.
- Sea bass contains B vitamins including B_6, B_{12}, niacin, riboflavin and thiamin.

Halibut

Halibut is a member of the flatfish family that is typically sold as steaks or fillets. Low in fat and calories, it is an excellent source of good-quality protein. It has a fairly mild taste making it amenable to a wide variety of flavourings. Delicious baked, grilled, pan-fried or steamed.

- Halibut provides some omega-3 fats plus the antioxidants zinc and selenium.

Trout

Closely related to salmon, trout are mainly freshwater fish – rainbow trout are most widely available. Sea trout are brown trout that migrate. Like salmon, trout is often farmed but it is generally considered low in toxins and a sustainable choice.

- Trout is a good source of omega-3 fats.
- Rich in B vitamins for a healthy nervous system and boosting energy.

Worried About Toxins and Fish?

We are often warned about consuming too much fish or shellfish due to potential harmful levels of mercury and other pollutants, including dioxins and PCBs (polychlorinated biphenyls). Fish can contain high levels of mercury as they absorb mercury from the water in which they live and from the organisms they consume.

Toxins are generally concentrated in the muscle and fat. The older the fish grows, the more toxins will accumulate in its tissues. Small fish at the lower end of the food chain tend to contain lower levels compared to larger fish higher up the food chain.

High levels of mercury in our bodies are known to cause damage to the nervous system. Mercury can cross the blood-brain barrier and placenta. However, seafood also contains high levels of selenium – this is an important antioxidant that can bind to methyl mercury preventing it from being absorbed readily by our bodies. For this reason most seafood, which is rich in selenium, is unlikely to be of real concern to our health. The fish with the lowest levels of methyl mercury include salmon, trout, haddock, sole, mackerel, sardines, herring (right)

and pollock. The main fish that are of concern are the larger carnivores such as shark, marlin, swordfish and (to a lesser extent) tuna. For this reason authorities recommend that pregnant women, women who intend to become pregnant, infants and children under 16 years of age should avoid eating shark, swordfish and marlin. For everyone else, it is recommended as a precaution that these fish are eaten occasionally (e.g. one portion of them a week).

Other pollutants such as dioxins and PCBs are an additional concern because of their carcinogenic properties. Typically wild fish are lower in these toxins than farmed stock, but even with farmed fish the health benefits of eating fish far outweigh the risks, particularly oily fish which contain lots of omega-3 fatty acids.

Salmon and Seafood Salad with Gremolata

LOW CARB

This is a delicious Mediterranean-style dish flavoured with a gremolata dressing – a mixture of crushed garlic, lemon, parsley and olive oil. You can vary the seafood in this salad – scallops, mussels, prawns and baby squid are all wonderful additions.

Prep: 10 mins/Cook: 15 mins

Ingredients (serves 4)

8 scallops, cleaned
250 g (9 oz) large raw prawns
2 tablespoons olive oil
Juice of ½ lemon
4 wild salmon fillets, boneless, skin on
Sea salt and freshly ground black pepper

Gremolata Dressing

Handful of fresh flat-leaf parsley, chopped
1 garlic clove, crushed
Juice and grated zest of 1 lemon
4 tablespoons olive oil
2 teaspoons manuka honey or xylitol

Method

1 Heat a sauté pan until hot. Drizzle the scallops and prawns with a little oil and season with salt and pepper. Cook the scallops for 1–2 minutes on each side and remove from the pan. Drain them on kitchen paper. Add the prawns to the pan and cook for 2–3 minutes each side until they turn pink and are cooked through. Remove the prawns from the pan and place them on the kitchen paper.

2 Sprinkle a little oil and lemon juice over the salmon fillets and pan-fry for 3–4 minutes, turning them once. Remove from the heat and leave to cool.

3 Combine all the dressing ingredients and season. Arrange lamb's lettuce, watercress, spinach and tomatoes on a plate. Add the seafood and top with the salmon. Drizzle over the dressing and serve.

RICH IN OMEGA-3 FOR A HEALTHY HEART	
Calories (per serving)	460
Protein	46 g
Total fat	28.2 g
of which saturated fat	4.5 g
Carbohydrates	5.6 g
of which sugars	4.3 g
Vitamins/minerals	A, C, B, potassium, zinc

Can I Eat Tinned Fish?

While it is preferable to choose fresh, unprocessed foods, tinned fish can be a useful and healthy storecupboard ingredient. Popular tinned fish include tuna, mackerel, sardines, herring, salmon and pilchards. These are all oily fish valuable for their omega-3 content. Tinned fish can be a convenient, cheap alternative to fresh fish, which is not always available.

Tinned tuna (unlike other tinned fish) is lower in omega-3 fats than fresh fish. This is because tuna loses a lot of its essential fatty acids when it goes through the food processing system to be tinned, so a fresh tuna steak would be a better choice. Tinned 'light' tuna,

normally made from skipjack tuna, poses a lower risk in terms of exposure to mercury toxins than fresh yellowfin or albacore tuna. So if you wish to eat tinned tuna, ideally choose skipjack.

When selecting tinned fish, choose products tinned in water, brine or olive oil rather than in sunflower oil. Sunflower oil is a polyunsaturated fat which is more prone to triggering free-radical damage in the body and promoting inflammation.

Tinned salmon is often packed in its own oil, meaning you may be getting the benefit of some extra omega-3 fatty acids. Tinned salmon also includes the fish bones which are softened during the canning process making them safe to eat. These bones provide calcium. For example, an 85-g (3-oz) serving of salmon has over half the calcium found in a 227-ml (8-fl oz) glass of cow's milk. Tinned sardines including their bones are another excellent source of calcium. If the tinned fish is packed in tomato sauce, you'll also be getting plenty of lycopene – a phytochemical known for its antioxidant and anti-cancer benefits – but choose one which is low in sugar and other additives.

Top Omega-3 Sources

If you are looking to optimize your intake of omega-3 fats, then it is best to consume fish rich in EPA (eicosapentaenoic acid) and DHA (docosahexaenoic acid) two to three times a week. For some inflammatory and autoimmune conditions you may benefit from a higher level. This table will help you to select the best sources:

High omega-3 fish with > 500 mg of omega-3 per serving (100 g/3½ oz)

- Mackerel
- Sardines
- Coho and sockeye salmon
- Trout
- Tinned albacore tuna
- Tinned wild Alaskan salmon
- Tinned sardines
- Tinned skinless pink salmon.

Medium omega-3 fish with 150–500 mg of omega-3 per serving (100 g/3½ oz)

- Haddock
- Cod
- Hake
- Halibut
- Prawns
- Sole
- Plaice
- Perch
- Bass
- Swordfish
- Oysters
- Alaskan king crab
- Farmed salmon.

Lower omega-3 fish with < 150 mg of omega-3 per serving (100 g/3½ oz)

- Mahi mahi
- Skate
- Bluefin tuna
- Monkfish
- Red snapper
- Grouper.

Left: A portion of broiled wild sockeye salmon is a tasty way of ensuring you get plenty of healthy omega-3 fats in your diet.

Shellfish

Shellfish is important to include in your diet since it is extremely rich in nutrients. It also provides fat-soluble vitamins A, D, E and K, as well as B vitamins to boost energy production. There are a vast range of options including squid, octopus, clams, crab, lobster, prawns, scallops and oysters. Allergy to shellfish is relatively common.

Nutrition: Shellfish contains zinc, copper, selenium, magnesium, potassium, phosphorus and omega-3. **Benefits:** Reduces the risk of heart attacks and strokes, and keeps the immune system healthy.

Prawns

Prawns are high in muscle-building protein, omega-3 fats and are an excellent source of betaine, a nutrient necessary for improving liver function and maintaining healthy levels of homocysteine, a common amino acid found in the blood.

- Prawns contain B_{12} to promote healthy nerves and boost energy levels.
- Prawns are rich in selenium and copper.

Mussels

Mussels are particularly high in iodine, which helps to regulate thyroid function and may reduce the risk of breast cancer.

- A useful energy-boosting food, mussels are rich in folate and B_{12}, and important for maintaining healthy red blood cells. A bowlful of mussels easily provides all your daily B_{12} needs and over half of your iodine requirements.

Lobster

There are numerous varieties of lobster, such as the European and the larger American (including the famous Maine).

- Lobsters provide plenty of protein with less cholesterol, calories and saturated fat than beef and pork. They also contain calcium for healthy nerve function and bone health. The vitamin E in lobster helps to protect cells from damage.

Crab

This popular crustacean is high in protein and low in calories – only 128 calories in 100 g (3½ oz) – and in saturated fat.

- Crab contains trace elements of selenium and chromium as well as calcium, copper and zinc.
- Crab contains lots of omega-3, which has anti-inflammatory properties so may be good for those with arthritis.

Oysters

Fresh oysters are high in protein, zinc and omega-3 fatty acids. Oysters also contain beneficial amounts of the amino acid tyrosine, which helps to support thyroid function and adrenal health. It may also help to improve mood.

- The high zinc levels in oysters are good for reproductive health and sexual function, particularly in men.

Mediterranean Chilli and Herb Prawns

HIGH PROTEIN

Succulent king prawns marinated in a herb dressing and pan-fried with chilli make this a protein-packed meal that is quick and easy to prepare. For plenty of flavour marinate the prawns in the dressing for one to two hours, or overnight. Serve with a simple salad for a quick lunch or Cauliflower Rice (see page 115) for a more substantial meal.

Prep: 2 hrs 25 mins/Cook: 5 mins

Ingredients (serves 4)
24 large raw prawns, peeled
1 red chilli, deseeded and sliced
2 garlic cloves, sliced
4 spring onions, sliced
1 teaspoon coconut oil

Dressing
2 tablespoons capers
1 anchovy
Handful of mint leaves
Handful of coriander leaves
Handful of parsley leaves
3 tablespoons balsamic or sherry vinegar
6 tablespoons extra virgin olive oil
Salt and freshly ground black pepper

Method
1 To make the dressing, place all the ingredients in a mini liquidizer or food processor and pulse until smooth.

2 Place the prawns in a shallow dish with the chilli, garlic and spring onions and pour over half of the dressing. Cover the dish and leave the prawns to marinate in the refrigerator for 1–2 hours, or overnight.

3 Heat the coconut oil in a frying pan. Add the prawns with their dressing and cook for 2–3 minutes until they are cooked through and look pink.

4 Serve with a salad and the rest of the dressing, stir-fry vegetables or cauliflower rice.

ENERGIZING AND BOOSTS MUSCLES	
Calories (per serving)	158
Protein	5.8 g
Total fat	14.6 g
of which saturated fat	2.6 g
Carbohydrates	0.5 g
of which sugars	0.4 g
Vitamins/minerals E, B, selenium, iron, zinc	

Vegetables

Vegetables are an essential source of antioxidants, vitamins and minerals. The fibre content is important for your digestive health and regulating blood sugar. They are a vital component of any diet and consuming a wide variety of colourful vegetables daily helps to keep you fit and healthy. The only vegetables excluded from the Paleo diet are pulses. For anyone following an autoimmune Paleo diet, the nightshade family of vegetables are also avoided.

If you suffer from digestive symptoms, it is a good idea to consume cooked rather than raw vegetables. Admittedly, cooking does destroy certain vitamins such as vitamin C, polyphenols and enzymes. However, cooking helps to break down the cellular structure making nutrients more bioavailable. For example, carotenoids are more readily absorbed in cooked vegetables than in raw. Ideally eat a combination of both cooked and raw vegetables every day. As green leafy vegetables are particularly rich in nutrients and low in carbohydrates it is a good idea to include plenty of them in your daily diet.

Below: Aim to include a colourful selection of vegetables in your daily diet.

Health Benefits of Vegetables

 Eye health: Many vegetables are valuable sources of vitamin C and the carotenoids lutein and zeaxanthin. Lutein and zeaxanthin are primary antioxidants that function in several regions of the eye, including the retina and the macula. A diet rich in vegetables can help to prevent age-related macular degeneration and reduce the risk of cataracts.

 Skin health: Loaded with antioxidants to protect the skin from damage, vegetables also provide plenty of vitamin C to help the body make collagen, an essential protein for glowing skin. Vegetables also provide the pigment beta-carotene. Beta-carotene can protect your skin against sun damage. Beta-carotene is converted to vitamin A in the body, an essential vitamin for mucosal health.

 Colon health: Leafy greens like kale and mustard greens and other brassicas, including broccoli and cabbage, have been shown to help protect against colon cancer.

 Weight loss: Vegetables are rich in fibre, an important substance for weight loss because it keeps you feeling full and helps to control your feelings of hunger. Fibre can also help to balance blood sugar by slowing the absorption of carbohydrates into the bloodstream.

 Bone health: Vegetables, particularly leafy greens, provide essential minerals for strong and healthy bones including calcium, magnesium, phosphorous and vitamin K.

Leafy Greens and Brassicas

Leafy greens are one of the most nutritious groups of vegetables. They are packed with an array of vitamins including vitamin C, E and K, as well as folate. They are particularly rich in minerals and provide a good source of bioavailable calcium. They also provide some omega-3 fatty acids in the form of alpha linolenic acid (ALA).

Nutrition: Dark leafy greens are very high in fibre and are an excellent source of carotenoids.

Benefits: Helps blood to clot, boosts the immune system and reduces the risk of heart disease and strokes.

Kale

Kale can be boiled, sautéed or steamed. Kale is rich in iron which is essential for energy. It is a good source of vitamin K that is important for heart and bone health.

- Per calorie, kale has more calcium than milk. Calcium prevents bone loss.
- Kale is a good source of vitamin C, which helps the production of collagen that is vital for cartilage and joint health.

Spinach

Spinach can be steamed or stir-fried. Rich in vitamins and minerals, spinach is a concentrated source of antioxidant carotenoids and flavonoids that are valued for their anti-inflammatory properties.

- Spinach is rich in vitamin K that is important for maintaining bone health. Vitamin K_1 helps to prevent the excessive activation of cells that break down bone.

Watercress

Watercress is an excellent source of the antioxidant vitamins A and C, as well as vitamin K. Eat watercress raw.

- Watercress is a rich source of isothiocyanates, compounds that have been shown to fight a wide range of cancers. 34 g (1¼ oz) of raw watercress contains over 1,900 mcg of lutein and zeaxanthin, which sustains eye health.

Broccoli

Broccoli is rich in the sulphur compound sulforaphane that has been shown to have cancer-preventative properties. It blocks a key destructive enzyme that damages cartilage so may prevent the development of osteoarthritis. Steam or stir-fry broccoli.

- Broccoli may help to balance blood sugar levels, as it contains both soluble fibre and chromium.

Cabbage

Cabbage juice is traditionally used as a remedy to relieve stomach ulcers due to its high phytonutrient content. It is rich in indole-3-carbinol, which may help to reduce the risk of stomach cancer. Cabbage can be stir-fried, steamed or used raw.

- Cabbage is a very good source of vitamin K, known to help prevent Alzheimer's disease.

Cauliflower

Cauliflower is a useful source of sulforophane, which maintains cell health. The glucosinolates in cauliflower reinforce detoxification pathways while its high antioxidant content helps to protect the body from free radical damage.

- Cauliflower provides choline, a nutrient known for its role in brain development, cognitive function and memory.

Spring Greens

Spring greens are a highly nutritious member of the brassica family closely related to kale and cabbage.

- Spring greens are a very good source of folate, which is important in DNA synthesis and protection of the baby during pregnancy.
- Rich in vitamins C and A, they help sustain a healthy immune system.

Turnip Greens

A member of the brassica family, turnip greens are rich in vitamin C, important for production of collagen, which provides structure to skin and hair.

- Turnip greens are very rich in iron for energy production.
- Turnip greens provide nitrate that has been shown to improve muscle oxygenation during exercise.

Swiss Chard

Like beetroot, chard is a valuable source of phytonutrients called betalains, which provide antioxidant, anti-inflammatory and detoxification benefits.

- Swiss chard has calcium, magnesium and vitamin K for healthy bones.
- A good source of manganese and zinc that help to prevent damage from chronic disease.

Why Eat Lettuce?

Don't overlook the nutritional benefits of lettuce. Cos, butterhead Little Gem and iceberg are just some of the most popular varieties. While iceberg is not particularly nutritious, other varieties – particularly cos– are packed with vitamins and minerals, fibre and phytonutrients that benefit health.

- Cos lettuce is particularly rich in vitamin C, beta-carotene, folate and potassium – all nutrients that have a positive effect on heart health.
- Lettuce is low in calories and high in fibre so can help you maintain a healthy weight and support the digestive system.

Tangy `Cheese` Kale Crisps

LOW CALORIE

Crunchy kale crisps make a healthy snack and are an ideal alternative to conventional high-fat processed potato crisps. You can bake these in an oven or, if you have a dehydrator, dehydrate them until crispy.

Prep: 20 mins/Cook: 25 mins

Ingredients (serves 8)

35 g (1¼ oz) sunflower seeds, soaked for
    2 hours then drained
40 g (1½ oz) cashew nuts, soaked for
    2 hours then drained
4 sun-dried tomatoes in oil, drained
½ red pepper, deseeded and chopped
½ teaspoon garlic salt
1 shallot, chopped
2 tablespoons nutritional yeast flakes
2 soft large dates, chopped
2 tablespoons lemon juice
2 tablespoons water
2 tablespoons apple cider vinegar
250 g (9 oz) bag of chopped kale

GREAT FOR STRONG HEALTHY BONES	
Calories (per serving)	96
Protein	4.9 g
Total fat	6.4 g
of which saturated fat	1.0 g
Carbohydrates	4.4 g
of which sugars	1.6 g
Vitamins/minerals	K, C, A, calcium, copper

Method

1 Blend all the ingredients except the kale to form a thick paste.

2 Place the kale in a bowl and pour over the sauce. Work thoroughly with your hands to ensure the kale is entirely coated in the sauce.

3 To dehydrate, place the kale on a non-stick mesh sheet and dehydrate for 4–6 hours. Then flip the kale over, place on the mesh sheet and dehydrate for a further 6–8 hours until crisp.

4 For an oven-baked version: preheat the oven to 150°C (300°F, gas mark 2). Place the kale on a lined baking sheet and bake for 15–20 minutes. Carefully turn the kale over and cook for a further 5 minutes until it is crisp.

5 Store the crisps in an airtight container for two to three days.

Cruciferous Vegetables and Goitrogens

Cruciferous vegetables are those in the Brassicaceae family. They are also known as Cruciferae (meaning 'cross-bearing') because of the shape of their flowers, whose four petals resemble a cross. They include cauliflower, cabbage, garden cress, pak choi, broccoli, Brussels sprouts and other green leaf vegetables.

Goitrogens are compounds found in cruciferous vegetables and some other vegetables and fruits. They have been shown to suppress the function of the thyroid by interfering with iodine uptake. Iodine is an essential mineral needed for the production of thyroid hormones T4 (thyroxine) and T3 (triiodothyronine). People with Hashimoto's or Grave's disease (autoimmune thyroid conditions) or hypothyroidism are sometimes advised to avoid consumption of cruciferous vegetables for this reason. However, there is little scientific research to suggest that eating cruciferous vegetables will cause a decrease in thyroid function in the absence of iodine deficiency.

As cruciferous vegetables are highly nutritious and have been linked to many health benefits, they should form a significant part of your diet. If you do have a thyroid condition or disorder, it is a good idea to ensure your diet is rich in the necessary minerals for thyroid hormone production, especially iron, selenium and zinc, and also consume iodine-rich foods, such as fish and sea vegetables (see page 128), regularly.

Most forms of cooking reduce goitrogen levels so if you are concerned about your thyroid function or you do have a disorder then you may be advised to lightly steam cruciferous vegetables rather than eating them raw.

Cauliflower Rice

HEALTHY HEART

Using cauliflower to create a rice is a delicious low-carb alternative to using grains. Cauliflower rice can be used in both raw and cooked dishes and works beautifully with Asian flavours.

Prep: 15 mins/Cook: 5 mins

Ingredients (serves 4)

1 medium head cauliflower, 500 g (18 oz)
1 tablespoon coconut oil
1 small onion, finely chopped
1 piece of fresh root ginger, grated
1–2 tablespoons coconut aminos
 or tamari
Drizzle of fish sauce
Drizzle of rice vinegar
Handful of chopped coriander leaves
Handful of chopped basil
Handful of chopped mint
Salt and freshly ground black pepper

Method

1 Place the cauliflower in a food processor and pulse until finely chopped so it looks like little rice size pieces.

2 Add the coconut oil to a large frying pan and sauté the onion and ginger. Add the cauliflower and season. Place the lid on and steam-fry for 5 minutes. Once softened, add the aminos, fish sauce, vinegar and herbs, and your rice is ready to serve.

SUPPORTS THE DIGESTIVE SYSTEM	
Calories (per serving)	82
Protein	3.9 g
Total fat	3.7 g
of which saturated fat	3 g
Carbohydrates	10.8 g
of which sugars	2.3 g
Vitamins/minerals	A, B, C, D, calcium

Non-starchy Vegetables

There are a variety of other non-starchy vegetables that are equally nutritious. They typically come from the stem, flower or flower bud rather than actual leaves. Here are just a few examples. Aim to include a wide variety of these tasty vegetables in your diet to optimize the range of nutrients you receive.

Nutrition: Non-starchy vegetables are high in fibre, vitamins and phytochemicals, and low in calories.
Benefits: Aids digestion, may improve memory, helps to keep the heart healthy and lowers blood pressure.

Asparagus

The fleshy green succulent spears of asparagus are readily available in spring. Asparagus can be good for digestive health as it is rich in inulin, a type of prebiotic fibre that encourages the growth of beneficial gut bacteria.

- Known for its anti-inflammatory, antioxidant properties, asparagus contains vitamin C, beta-carotene, vitamin E and the minerals zinc, manganese and selenium.
- Asparagus contains a significant amount of the antioxidant glutathione which helps the body to rid itself of toxins.
- Asparagus is a good source of B vitamins including folate to help improve cognitive function.

Fennel

The crisp fennel bulb can be sautéed, stewed, braised, grilled or eaten raw.

- Fennel is rich in a range of phytonutrients including anethole which can help reduce inflammation and the risk of certain cancers. It is a very good source of folate, an important B vitamin during pregnancy, and potassium that helps to lower high blood pressure.

Globe Artichokes

Globe artichokes can be boiled or steamed and are a good source of fibre that is beneficial for digestive health.

- Globe artichokes are packed with phytonutrients such as quercetin, rutin, gallic acid and cynarin, which help protect against conditions like heart disease, liver dysfunction, high cholesterol and diabetes.

Celery

Celery contains a range of antioxidant nutrients, including vitamin C, beta-carotene and manganese, and is particularly high in phenolic antioxidants known for their anti-inflammatory benefits.

- The pectin-based polysaccharides in celery are good for stomach health.
- A useful source of vitamin K for a healthy heart and bones.

Allium Family

Alliums (also known as the onion family) are known for their powerful aroma. This is due to the concentration of sulphur compounds, which have been shown to have numerous health benefits including helping the body to rid itself of toxins. Alliums are rich in important minerals such as selenium, iron and manganese.

Nutrition: Alliums are rich in antioxidants, vitamins C, A, B and K, and many minerals.
Benefits: Can protect the heart, lower cholesterol, increase bone density and are powerful anti-inflammatories.

Leeks

Leeks contain a range of B vitamins which can be good for heart health. They also strengthen the neural system of babies developing in the womb. Leeks contain the flavonoid kaempferol that helps to protect blood vessel linings from damage.

- Leeks contain vitamins A and K, and healthy amounts of folic acid, niacin, riboflavin, magnesium and thiamin.

Garlic

Garlic contains the sulphur compound known as allicin that is responsible for its distinctive smell.

- Garlic is low in calories.
- A rich source of vitamin C, vitamin B$_6$ and manganese and other trace nutrients.
- Garlic supplementation has been shown to strengthen the immune system and it is valued for its anti-microbial properties.

Red Onions

Red onions are a rich source of quercetin, a bioflavonoid known for its antioxidant and anti-histamine properties.

- Onions are a rich source of chromium, a trace mineral that can help control glucose levels making it beneficial for people with diabetes.
- Red onions provide significant amounts of vitamin C and vitamin B_6.

White Onions

A good source of flavonoids and sulphur-containing nutrients. The high sulphur content of onions may help to strengthen connective tissue and bone as well as benefiting cardiovascular health.

- Onions provide B vitamins including biotin, important for skin and hair.
- Onions contain copper to maintain healthy red blood cells.

Chives

Chives are a nutrient-dense herb packed with a range of vitamins and minerals including folate, choline, calcium, magnesium, phosphorus and potassium.

- Chives are believed to have cancer-protective properties.
- The choline in chives is an important nutrient that helps memory and the structure of cellular membranes.

Roots and Tubers

Roots and tubers are generally higher in starch than other vegetables. The glycaemic index (GI) varies – carrots, for example, are relatively low GI while beetroot are higher. These foods contribute the main part of your carbohydrate intake on a Paleo diet. Roots and tubers can be roasted, boiled, steamed, fried and baked.

Nutrition: Roots and tubers are high in fibre and are excellent sources of vitamins, minerals and antioxidants. **Benefits:** Helps to keep the heart healthy, reduces the risk of heart disease and lowers blood pressure.

Sweet Potato

Orange-fleshed sweet potatoes are rich in beta-carotene which boosts our levels of vitamin A. The purple-fleshed variety is full of anthocyanins which have antioxidant and anti-inflammatory properties.

- Sweet potatoes provide plenty of vitamin C and B vitamins, and may increase levels of adiponectin that helps to improve insulin metabolism.

Carrot

A popular root vegetable, carrots are particularly rich in carotenoids and other antioxidants that are known to be good for cardiovascular health.

- Carotenoids are also important to maintain healthy vision and reduce the risk of cataracts and glaucoma.
- Carrots contain soluble fibre and may offer protection against colon cancer.

Beetroot

A popular root for boosting heart health and athletic performance. Beetroot is rich in nitrates, which are converted into nitric oxide in your body. Nitric oxide helps to relax blood vessels, improving blood flow and lowering blood pressure.

- Beetroot is a unique source of betaine, a nutrient with anti-inflammatory and detoxifying properties.

Parsnips

This sweet root vegetable contains more calories and starch than carrots, but is rich in essential nutrients and fibre.

- Parsnips are packed with vitamin C that aids the immune system and keeps teeth and gums healthy.
- Parsnips are rich in B vitamins and vitamins K and E to help maintain a healthy heart.

Celeriac

A member of the celery family, celeriac can be used raw or cooked and is popular mashed to replace potatoes.

- Celeriac is a very good source of vitamin K, which is particularly important for promoting bone and heart health. To aid absorption of this fat-soluble vitamin, add a little fat to the dish when preparing and eating celeriac.

Beetroot, Carrot and Pear Coleslaw with Lime Dressing

HIGH FIBRE

A vibrant colourful salad, sweet and tangy with the addition of the Asian-style dressing. It is delicious served with meat or fish. Use a spiralizer if you want to create long noodle strips. Alternatively, you can use a mandoline or food processor to create long strips rapidly. The salad can be dressed ahead of time to intensify the flavours.

Prep: 15 mins

Ingredients (serves 4)

2 carrots, spiralized or cut into julienne
1 large beetroot, spiralized or cut into
   julienne
¼ fennel bulb, cored and cut into
   long strips
1 shallot, finely chopped
1 pear, grated or cut into long strips
1 teaspoon nigella seeds/cumin seeds

Dressing

½ teaspoon grated root ginger
2 tablespoons tamari
1 tablespoon lime juice
2 tablespoons rice wine vinegar
1 teaspoon honey
¼ red chilli, deseeded and diced

Method

1 Place all the spiralized or cut vegetables into a large bowl.

2 Whisk all the dressing ingredients together until smooth. Drizzle over the salad and toss completely. Store in the refrigerator until ready to serve.

GOOD FOR A HEALTHY HEART	
Calories (per serving)	64
Protein	1.5 g
Total fat	0.3 g
of which saturated fat	0.1 g
Carbohydrates	13.2 g
of which sugars	12.9 g
Vitamins/minerals	C, B, A, K, manganese

Squash

Summer and winter squashes are members of the Cucurbitaceae family and relatives of both the melon and the cucumber. They are sometimes also called the gourd family. Squashes come in numerous varieties, both winter and summer, with many that are good to eat. Some varieties, such as courgette, also produce edible flowers.

Nutrition: Squashes are very nutritious and are high in vitamins A, C, B and omega-3 fatty acids.
Benefits: Keeps the heart healthy, regulates blood sugar levels and are powerful anti-inflammatories.

Courgette

A low-calorie, low-carb vegetable that is delicious eaten raw or cooked. Very popular for making low-carb noodles too.

- Courgettes are a good source of magnesium and potassium, which can help to balance fluid levels.
- They are also rich in vitamin C and the carotenoid lutein, both beneficial for their antioxidant properties.

Pumpkin

Pumpkins are very rich in vitamin A and carotenoids that are important for skin and eye health. They are valued for their cancer-protective benefits.

- Pumpkin is a good source of fibre and low in calories. This helps you feel full for longer – ideal for weight management.
- This squash is high in potassium, so replenishes electrolytes after exercise.

Butternut Squash

Butternut squash, a common winter variety, is extremely rich in vitamin A.

- Butternut squash is incredibly rich in vitamins A, C and E. These antioxidants protect against cell damage and are good for skin, hair and eyes.
- A good source of potassium, butternut squash is useful for maintaining healthy blood pressure.

Spaghetti Squash

Spaghetti squash gets its name from the fact that when it is cooked, the inside flesh pulls out of the shell in long strands, resembling spaghetti pasta.

- Spaghetti squash is rich in a range of vitamins including vitamins C, A and B vitamins.
- This squash is a good source of manganese to keep bones healthy.

Acorn Squash

Acorn squash is an excellent source of vitamin C that helps to maintain a healthy immune system.

- Acorn squash is very high in dietary fibre. About 245 g (8¾ oz) cooked squash contains 6 g of fibre and 83 calories. It aids digestive health, lowers high cholesterol and also regulates the levels of blood sugar in the body.

Paleo Pumpkin Tart

HIGH FIBRE

This is a healthy alternative to the traditional pumpkin pie. You can use tinned pumpkin purée if you wish, or simply steam pumpkin or butternut squash and then process it in a food processor. This recipe has a spoonful of cacao powder added to the base for additional flavour. Serve with coconut cream or yogurt.

Prep: 20 mins/Cook: 1 hr

Ingredients (serves 8)

Base

250 g (9 oz) pecan nuts
1 tablespoon raw cacao powder
60 g (2 oz) pitted soft dates
1 tablespoon vanilla extract
1 tablespoon coconut oil
1 tablespoon honey

Filling

400 g (14 oz) pumpkin or butternut
    squash purée
2 eggs
125 ml (4 fl oz) coconut cream
1 teaspoon ground cinnamon
1 teaspoon allspice
1 teaspoon ground ginger
1 tablespoon vanilla extract
1 tablespoon lucuma powder, optional
60 g (2 oz) coconut sugar
Dusting of raw cacao powder, to decorate
2 tablespoons pecan nuts, optional

Method

1 Preheat the oven to 180°C (350°F, gas mark 4).

2 Place the pecans in a food processor and process until very fine. Add the cacao, dates, vanilla, oil and honey and process until the mixture comes together.

3 Press the mixture into a greased springform loose-based 20-cm (8-inch) cake tin.

PACKED WITH ANTIOXIDANTS	
Calories (per serving)	374
Protein	6.1 g
Total fat	30.2 g
of which saturated fat	8.0 g
Carbohydrates	19.9 g
of which sugars	15.1 g
Vitamins/minerals	A, C, B, potassium, iron

4 Place all the filling ingredients in a liquidizer and process until smooth. Pour the mixture into the cake tin on top of the pecan base and bake for 1 hour until the filling has puffed up in the centre and turned light golden.

5 Serve the pumpkin tart warm or cold. Decorate with a dusting of cacao powder and/or the pecans, if desired.

Sea Vegetables

The numerous health benefits deriving from sea vegetables may be due to their fucoidan content. Fucoidans are starch-like sulphur-containing molecules or polysaccharides. Known for their anti-inflammatory and anti-cancer benefits, they also appear to support the immune system and promote cardiovascular health.

Nutrition: Sea vegetables are an excellent source of iodine and are packed with minerals and vitamins. **Benefits:** Purifies the blood and lowers blood pressure, may improve memory and keeps the skin healthy.

Nori

Best known as the outer wrap for sushi, nori is an edible red seaweed that is popular in east Asia, especially Japan. Use to make Paleo sushi rolls, add to soups or simply delicious as a snack toasted with a little oil.

- Nori provides protein, omega-3 fats and is a useful source of iron and calcium. It has a low iodine content.

Wakame

Wakame is an edible brown seaweed common in Asian cuisines. To prepare, soak for 15 minutes until soft, drain and rinse. Heat gently or simply add to salads raw.

- Wakame contains magnesium and calcium for bone health.
- This seaweed contains iron and vitamins to help keep the skin healthy and boost the immune system.

Arame

An edible brown seaweed that is rich in iodine. This thin wiry sea vegetable is sweeter and milder in taste than many others – delicious in salads and soups.

- Arame contains lots of fibre that helps the digestive system and detoxification, and may lower cholesterol.
- Arame provides a good source of vitamin A, calcium, iron and magnesium.

Dulse

Red or purple in colour, dulse is a valuable source of iodine and minerals, particularly phosphorous, iron and potassium. It is also rich in antioxidants, which serve a protective role in the body.

- Dulse is a good source of protein and fibre to maintain blood sugar balance.
- The polysaccharides content in dulse helps the body to eliminate toxins.

Hijiki

Similar to arame, hijiki is bolder in flavour, with anise-like undertones. Some studies have shown that it can contain high levels of arsenic – for this reason, only eat hijiki if it comes from a certified organic source.

- Rich in iron to boost energy levels.
- Hijiki contains calcium and magnesium to keep the nervous system healthy and to strengthen bones.

Tom Yum Soup with Dulse

HIGH PROTEIN

Tom yum paste is readily available in supermarkets. It contains a delicious combination of galangal, lemongrass, chilli, garlic and lime. This is a simple creamy soup, packed with protein because of the prawns and with plenty of minerals thanks to the addition of dulse.

Prep: 15 mins/Cook: 12 mins

Ingredients (serves 4)

40 g (1½ oz) dulse fronds
2 x 400 g (14 oz) cans whole coconut milk
1 tablespoon tom yum paste
Juice of ½ lime
Small pinch of saffron threads
Handful of spinach leaves
2 spring onions, shredded
200 g (7 oz) cooked king prawns
Coriander, chopped, to garnish

Method

1 Place the dulse in water and soak for 10 minutes. Drain.

2 Pour the coconut milk into a medium pan and heat gently. Add the dulse, tom yum paste, lime juice and saffron.

3 Stir well and bring to a gentle boil. Reduce the heat and simmer for 1 minute. Just before serving add the spinach leaves, spring onions and prawns and cook for 1 minute to heat through.

4 Spoon the soup into bowls and sprinkle over the chopped coriander leaves before serving.

EXCELLENT FOR BOOSTING ENERGY LEVELS	
Calories (per serving)	120
Protein	11.48 g
Total fat	4.34 g
of which saturated fat	1.20 g
Carbohydrates	8.56 g
of which sugars	5.15 g
Vitamins/minerals	B, iron, selenium, zinc

Nuts and Seeds

Nuts and seeds are included in a Paleo diet but they are typically avoided by anyone following an autoimmune programme. This is because they may promote inflammation if eaten in excess.

Nuts can be high in phytic acid, which binds to minerals in food (especially iron and zinc) and prevents us from absorbing them. Phytic acid interferes with enzymes that we need to digest our food. Levels of phytate may be reduced by soaking and dehydrating nuts before eating them. Nut flours do not contain much phytic acid. This is because the flour

is made from blanched nuts and the phytic acid is found mostly in the skin of the nuts. Avoid nuts packaged or roasted in oil or containing added sugars; instead, eat them raw or lightly roasted.

While seeds (pumpkin, sunflower, sesame, chia, flaxseed, etc.) feature in a Paleo diet, processed seed oils do not. These seed oils are high in omega-6 polyunsaturated fats, and a significant disproportion between omega-3 and omega-6 fatty acid intake can cause inflammation. Cold pressed nut and seed oils can be used in dressings but they should not be heated as their nutritional content may be damaged.

Nuts and seeds, however, are packed with nutrients and provide plenty of protein, vitamins and minerals. They also provide some healthy monounsaturated and omega-3 fatty acids, which can be good for heart health. Their high fibre and protein content makes them very satisfying. Some nuts and seeds also contain plant sterols, which can help to lower high LDL cholesterol.

Health Benefits of Nuts and Seeds

 Brain health: Nuts and seeds are a good source of zinc and magnesium that are important for the production of brain neurotransmitters and omega-3 fats to assist cognitive function.

 Sleep: Many nuts and seeds are rich in calcium and magnesium that help relax the muscles and nervous system. Some provide tryptophan, an amino acid that your body converts into serotonin, which in turn is converted into melatonin, the 'sleep hormone'.

 Heart health: Nuts are rich in a range of heart protective nutrients including vitamin E, B vitamins, magnesium, potassium, omega-3 and monounsaturated fats. A good source of fibre and plant sterols, which can help to lower high LDL cholesterol.

Men's health: These foods are rich in zinc, which is important for prostate health, male fertility and the production of testosterone. Nuts and seeds also provide magnesium, which is very important for maintaining healthy levels of testosterone and also helping to keep the heart healthy.

 Skin health: All nuts and seeds are rich in vitamin E, an antioxidant that keeps your skin glowing. The omega-3 fats, selenium and zinc in some nuts and seeds are also good for the skin. Zinc, in particular, helps to maintain collagen, which keeps your skin smooth and soft.

Nuts

Nuts are an excellent source of energy, antioxidants, vitamins, minerals and essential omega-3 fatty acids. Nuts contain fibre, which can help to lower cholesterol and make you feel fuller for longer. Nuts also contain L-arginine, a substance that can help to make artery walls more flexible and less prone to blockages.

Nutrition: Nuts are packed with protein, vitamins, minerals, essential fats and fibre.
Benefits: Helps to lower cholesterol levels, protects against heart disease and may reduce the risk of strokes.

Almonds

Almonds are popular in Paleo baking recipes when ground up to form a flour.

- Almonds are high in monounsaturated fats, vitamin E, magnesium, potassium and fibre, all good for a healthy heart.
- They have been shown to help lower LDL cholesterol.
- The flavonoids found in almond skins help to stabilize blood sugar.

Hazelnuts

Also known as filberts or 'cobnuts', hazelnuts contain lots of minerals.

- Hazelnuts are high in folate that can help to maintain healthy levels of homocysteine and reduce the risk of neural tube defects in the foetus.
- These nuts are a good source of vitamin E that is important for the integrity of cell membranes and skin health.

Cashew Nuts

Cashew nuts are lower in fat than many other nuts and are a good source of heart-healthy monounsaturated fats.

- Cashew nuts are particularly rich in copper, a mineral important for iron utilization, the health of bone and connective tissue and also the production of the skin and hair pigment called melanin.

Brazil Nuts

Brazil nuts are rich in monounsaturated fats and vitamin E making them particularly good for the heart.

- Brazil nuts are one of the best food sources of selenium – just three will supply your daily recommended intake. Selenium is vital for immune function, hormone production, detoxification and antioxidant protection.

Pecan Nuts

Popular in desserts and pies, pecan nuts are particularly rich in phenolic antioxidants and monounsaturated fatty acids making them good for the heart.

- The antioxidant ellagic acid has been shown to possess anti-cancer properties.
- Pecans are a good source of B vitamins and protein, they can boost energy levels and balance blood sugar levels.

Macadamia Nuts

Macadamia nuts taste sweet and are a good source of energy.

- Macadamias have a beneficial fat profile, as they are very low in omega-6 fats and high in anti-inflammatory monounsaturated fats.
- These nuts provide palmitoleic acid, which has positive effects on blood lipids and is an effective skin moisturizer.

Walnuts

Walnuts are higher in omega-3 fats than other nuts. They also contain a number of neuroprotective compounds, including vitamin E, folate and antioxidants.

- If you suffer from herpes, you may want to avoid or limit walnuts, as their arginine content can deplete levels of the amino acid lysine, which can trigger recurrences of herpes.

Pistachios

Pistachios are packed with antioxidants, as well as containing healthy fats and the minerals selenium and iron.

- Pistachios have been shown to improve lipid levels and lower high LDL cholesterol.
- These nuts are a good source of lutein, beta-carotene and vitamin E. Lutein is important for vision and skin health.

Seeds

Small, but packed with an array of nutrients, seeds are a healthy addition to a Paleo diet. You can also soak and blend many seeds to create seed milks.

A valuable source of protein, seeds have a healthier ratio of omega-3 to 6 fatty acids compared to most nuts. Useful as a snack or an addition to dishes.

Nutrition: Seeds are packed with fibre, vitamins and minerals including zinc, iron, calcium and phosphorus.
Benefits: Strengthens bones, helps keep the immune system healthy and promotes healthy skin and hair.

Pumpkin Seeds

Pumpkin seeds are particularly valuable for their high levels of zinc and magnesium.

- Pumpkin seed oil is rich in natural phytoestrogens that may help alleviate menopausal symptoms.
- Good for men's prostate health, pumpkin seed extracts may play a role in treating benign enlargement of the prostate gland.

Sunflower Seeds

Sunflower seeds are an excellent source of vitamin E, the body's primary fat-soluble antioxidant. Vitamin E is known for its anti-inflammatory effects and plays a role in the prevention of cardiovascular disease.

- Sunflower seeds are a good source of magnesium that can help maintain healthy nerves and muscles and reduce the severity of asthma and migraines.

Flaxseed

Flaxseeds are available whole or ground. Whole flaxseeds can be used in baking while ground can be added to porridge, smoothies, sprinkled on to salads and mixed into pancake batters.

- Flaxseed is known for its high protein and fibre content, so is good for your digestive health, alleviating constipation and regulating blood sugar levels.

Sesame Seeds

Also available as tahini which is a sesame seed paste. Sesame seeds are an excellent source of copper, which may help to relieve the pain of arthritis.

- Sesame seeds contain magnesium and calcium for healthy bones.
- These seeds contain zinc, which is important for sex hormone production and fertility.

Pine Nuts

Pine nuts are not actually nuts, but are the seeds of pine trees. Delicious eaten raw or roasted, with a sweet nutty flavour.

- These seeds are rich in nutrients that help to boost energy.
- They may help with weight loss as they contain pinolenic acid, which triggers the release of an appetite-suppressing hormone known as cholecystokinin.

Chia Seeds

Chia seeds are tiny black seeds from the plant *Salvia hispanica*, a member of the mint family. It was prized as an energy fuel by the Aztecs. They are loaded with fibre, protein, omega-3 fatty acids and antioxidants. Because chia seeds are rich in soluble fibre, they can absorb ten to 12 times their weight in water. They should be soaked in water before they are eaten – if taken dry, you may have problems swallowing them. They are effective for balancing blood sugar and promoting weight loss, and are a good source of calcium, magnesium, phosphorus and protein to aid bone health. There are concerns that they may damage the gut lining so it is best to avoid them on an autoimmune Paleo diet, or observe a limit of 1 heaped tablespoon daily.

Raspberry Chia Dessert

HIGH FIBRE

A simple, protein-packed, omega-3-rich breakfast dessert. Soak the chia seeds overnight to make this a speedy healthy start to the day.

Prep: 15 mins/Soak: 15 mins

Ingredients (serves 1)

3 tablespoons chia seeds
250 ml (8 fl oz) almond milk
30 g (1 oz) raspberries
Pinch of ground cinnamon

Method

1 Put all the ingredients into a bowl. Stir constantly for 1 minute so that the seeds don't clump together.

2 You can either soak this overnight in the refrigerator or leave to soak for 15 minutes in the morning. When ready to serve, place in a liquidizer or process in a food processor to mash up the berries. Spoon into a glass and top with a few extra raspberries to serve.

KEEPS BONES HEALTHY AND STRONG	
Calories (per serving)	156
Protein	5.9 g
Total fat	9.5 g
of which saturated fat	0 g
Carbohydrates	17.9 g
of which sugars	0 g
Vitamins/minerals A, C, D, B, E, calcium, iron	

Fruits and Berries

Fruits are packed with an array of phytochemicals, antioxidants, vitamins and minerals as well as fibre to support health. Focus on low-sugar fruits to limit your intake of fructose, and avoid fruit juices.

Fruits are an important food group in the Paleo diet. While fresh fruit does contain more sugar than vegetables, most fruits are relatively low in glycaemic index (GI). Dried fruits tend to be high in sugars and glycaemic load (GL) so should only be eaten in small amounts. People with blood sugar imbalances or inflammatory conditions should avoid fruit juices, smoothies and dried fruit and limit fruit to around two portions a day. This will keep their fructose intake low.

Berries typically have the highest vitamin, mineral and antioxidant content, as well as being lower in sugar than other fruits. They are particularly rich in compounds called anthocyanins, which are a type of flavonoid shown to be beneficial for healthy ageing and reducing oxidative damage to the body caused by free radicals. To maximize your antioxidant benefits from fruits, choose organic, seasonal produce. Frozen fruit is a very healthy alternative when out of season.

Health Benefits of Fruits and Berries

 Brain health: Fruits such as berries are rich in flavonoids, especially anthocyanins, which have been shown to counteract cognitive decline and may help to reduce the risk of developing Parkinson's disease.

 Heart health: Fruits contain a wealth of phytochemicals, antioxidants, vitamins and minerals that help to protect the heart, lower blood pressure and reduce inflammation. Some fruits like apples contain pectin, a soluble fibre that can help to maintain healthy cholesterol levels.

 Cancer protective: Fruits are rich in a number of compounds such as ellagic acid and limonene that have been shown to possess anti-cancer properties. They are a good source of fibre and may help to reduce the risk of colon cancer too.

 Digestive health: Many fruits are excellent sources of soluble fibre, which helps regulate bowel movements and benefits digestive health. Green bananas are particularly rich in prebiotic fibre that encourages the growth of beneficial bacteria in the gut.

 Skin health: A good source of vitamin C, which helps your body to produce collagen, a protein that helps to keep your skin firm and elastic. Many fruits are also rich in carotenoids, which can help to protect the skin from damage including UV damage caused by exposure to the sun.

Berries

While all fruits and vegetables contain antioxidants, nutrient-rich berries are some of the best sources. They contain numerous powerful antioxidants, including anthocyanins, which gives them their vibrant colour. Known for their anti-inflammatory, anti-ageing benefits, berries are one of the best fruits to eat raw.

Nutrition: Berries are packed with powerful antioxidants, vitamin C, fibre and folate.
Benefits: Keeps skin and hair healthy, reduces the risk of arthritis, reduces inflammation and lowers cholesterol.

Blueberries

Known for their exceptional phytonutrient and antioxidant content, blueberries seem to be very good for the nervous system and brain health and may reduce the risk of cognitive decline and Alzheimer's.

- Blueberries are beneficial for the heart.
- They have been shown to improve lipid profiles and raise the level of beneficial HDL cholesterol.

Raspberries

An excellent source of vitamin C and phytonutrients, raspberries provide anti-inflammatory and antioxidant benefits.

- The ellagic acid found in raspberries has been shown to have anti-cancer properties.
- Other compounds in raspberries increase metabolism in our fat cells and balance blood sugar levels.

Strawberries

Strawberries are one of the best fruits from which to obtain vitamin C. They contain a wealth of phytonutrients including anti-ageing anthocyanins.

- Strawberries have potent anti-inflammatory properties and seem to help balance blood sugar too.
- A good source of manganese to keep the skin healthy.

Cranberries

Rich in vitamin C, cranberries provide anti-inflammatory benefits particularly for the cardiovascular and digestive systems.

- Cranberries help to prevent urinary tract infections. The phytochemicals in cranberries contain proanthocyanidins (PACs) that stop potential pathogenic bacteria from adhering to the lining of the urinary tract.

Blackberries

Rich in vitamin C and anthocyanins, blackberries are good for cognitive function. The high tannin content of blackberries may reduce intestinal inflammation and alleviate diarrhoea.

- Blackberries are a good source of vitamin K that helps blood clotting.
- They are a low-calorie high-fibre fruit and help with weight management.

Berry Ice Cream

ENERGIZING

A delicious dairy-free ice cream packed with vitamin C and antioxidants. The addition of macadamia nuts creates a wonderful creamy texture as well as providing plenty of protein and healthy fats. You can use frozen berries if you want to. To boost the antioxidant content even more, add a spoonful of superfood berry powder.

Prep: 20 mins/Freeze: 2 to 3 hrs

Ingredients (serves 6)

200 g (7 oz) macadamia nuts
25 ml (1 fl oz) pure pomegranate juice
2 teaspoons vanilla extract
1 tablespoon mixed superfood berry
   powder, optional
120 g (4 oz) mixed berries, fresh or frozen
1 tablespoon lemon juice
60 g (2 oz) xylitol or honey

Method

1 Place the nuts and juice in a high-speed liquidizer and process to combine them. Add the remaining ingredients and process until thick and smooth.

2 Pour the mixture into an ice-cream maker and churn according to the manufacturer's instructions. Or, pour into a freezerproof container and freeze for 30 minutes, then remove and mix well. Continue until firm, about 2–3 hours.

3 Soften the ice cream 15 minutes before serving. Serve with fresh berries and mint.

RICH IN ANTIOXIDANTS	
Calories (per serving)	288
Protein	3.0 g
Total fat	25.9 g
of which saturated fat	3.8 g
Carbohydrates	14.6 g
of which sugars	4.5 g
Vitamins/minerals	C, K, E, B, manganese

Super Berries

Berries are renowned for their health-promoting properties. As well as popular favourites like blueberries and raspberries, there are many others that are rich in an array of healthy phytonutrients, as well as other vitamins and minerals. These 'super berries' are available all year round in the form of powders, dried berries or juice.

Nutrition: Super berries contain vitamins A, C and B and are packed with antioxidants.
Benefits: Boosts energy levels, have anti-ageing properties and helps to keep the skin and eyes healthy.

Goji Berries

Also called wolfberries, goji berries are a popular superfood. They are a vibrant red and have a deliciously intense flavour.
- Rich in carotenoids, antioxidants that are particularly beneficial for skin and eyes.
- They are an extremely nutrient-dense food and surprisingly high in amino acids. This makes them a wonderfully energizing food choice.

Mulberries

The mulberry is predominantly found in subtropical areas of Africa, Asia and North America. As they have a short shelf life, they are commonly sun-dried.
- Mulberries are a popular anti-ageing fruit due to their high antioxidant levels.
- A good source of vitamin C, mulberries are also packed with other nutrients.
- Mulberries provide protein for energy.

Acai Berries

The acai berry is the fruit of a palm tree that grows in the rainforests of the Amazon and is known as 'the tree of life'.

- Acai berries are one of the most concentrated sources of antioxidants, known as anthocyanins, which have potent anti-ageing benefits.
- These berries are a good source of fibre, vitamins C and A, calcium and fats.

Camu Camu Berries

These berries grow on a small bush native to the swampy lowlands of Peru. They are similar in size to a cranberry and have a slightly sour, tangy flavour. Available as freeze-dried powder, camu camu berry is used in small amounts only.

- Camu camu berries are packed with vitamin C, which is helpful in preventing diseases including colds and flu.

Goldenberries

Also known as Cape gooseberries. The fresh berry looks like a small yellow-orange cherry surrounded with papery husks resembling a Chinese lantern. The harvested berries are sun-dried and have a citrus-like, slightly sweet-sour flavour.

- The berries contain a variety of vitamins, including vitamins A and C, and many B vitamins to boost energy levels.

Rosaceae Family

Fruits from the Rosaceae family include both apples, pears and some stone fruit including cherries, peaches and plums. While apples are typically available all year round, others like cherries and plums have a much shorter season. However, most of these fruits freeze well, making them available throughout the year.

Nutrition: These fruits are high in fibre and packed with carotenoids and other antioxidants and minerals.
Benefits: Lowers cholesterol, helps prevent high blood pressure and strokes and prevents constipation.

Apples

Apples contain an array of polyphenols, which are antioxidants and seem to help protect the heart as well as lowering the incidence of asthma.

- Apples are rich in soluble fibre pectin, so may help lower total and LDL cholesterol. Pectin can also help stabilize blood sugar levels and reduce cravings.
- They also stimulate healthy gut flora.

Pears

Pears contain lots of phytonutrient antioxidants, particularly in the skins. These protect against cell damage and have anti-inflammatory benefits.

- Pears are a very good source of fibre, they can help the blood sugar balance and digestion. As pear fibres bind bile acids, they can be helpful in improving cholesterol levels too.

Why Eat Cherries?

Cherries – and more specifically tart cherries – are often overlooked for their health benefits. Sweet cherries contain fibre, vitamin C, carotenoids and anthocyanins, each of which may help to play a role in cancer prevention. Tart cherries are anti-inflammatory and may help to lower your risk of gout attacks and reduce the pain and inflammation associated with osteoarthritis. They are also beneficial in improving recovery after exercise. Cherries provide a natural source of melatonin to aid sleep. Tart cherries may help your body to metabolize fat and glucose so assisting you to lose weight. Tart cherries are available either dried or as a concentrated juice throughout the year.

Plums

The high fibre in prunes (dried plums) helps alleviate constipation, lowers cholesterol and improves digestive health. Prunes' insoluble fibre provides food for the 'friendly' bacteria in the large intestine.

- Fresh plums are a good source of vitamin C, improving the absorption of iron.
- Plums are rich in phenols which have antioxidant protective properties.

Peaches

Peaches are a good source of beta-carotene that the body converts to vitamin A, which benefits skin and eye health and the immune system.

- Peaches are rich in vitamin C and a number of phenols, vitamins and minerals essential for heart health including potassium, magnesium, folate, choline and vitamin E.

Nectarines

Related to peaches nutritionally, nectarines contain a slightly higher concentration of certain minerals like iron, phosphorus and potassium. They are also a useful source of vitamins A and C and the B vitamins.

- One medium nectarine contains around 285 mg of potassium. Potassium helps the body to maintain a healthy blood pressure and balances fluid levels.

Apricots

Apricots are rich in beta-carotene, vitamin C and fibre. The presence of carotenoids and xanthophylls may help to protect eyesight from age-related damage.

- Apricots also contain catechins, which have strong anti-inflammatory and anti-cancer properties.
- Dried apricots are rich in fibre making them ideal for alleviating constipation.

Apricot and Peach Crisp

HIGH FIBRE

This delicious Paleo fruit dessert is similar to crumble but much healthier. You can use this nutritious topping for all types of fruit including bags of frozen fruits when fresh are not available.

Prep: 20 mins/Cook: 50 mins

Ingredients (serves 6)

10 apricots, stoned and sliced
4 ripe nectarines or peaches, stoned
   and sliced
150 g (5 oz) almonds or almond flour
2 tablespoons ground flaxseed
Pinch of sea salt
1 tablespoon ground cinnamon
1 tablespoon ground ginger
4 tablespoons coconut oil melted
2 tablespoons honey
100 g (3½ oz) chopped pecan nuts

Method

1 Preheat the oven to 180°C (350°F, gas mark 4). Place the apricots and peaches in a baking dish.

2 Grind the whole almonds, if using, until very fine in a food processor. Transfer to a large bowl and combine with the flaxseeds, salt and ground spices. Mix the oil and honey together, then using your hands, work this into the almond mixture to form a crumbly dough. Gently mix in the pecans. Sprinkle the topping over the fruit.

3 Bake in the oven for 40–50 minutes until golden and crisp.

HELPS TO PROTECT YOUR EYESIGHT	
Calories (per serving)	390
Protein	8.2 g
Total fat	32.5 g
of which saturated fat	7.3 g
Carbohydrates	16.4 g
of which sugars	15.5 g
Vitamins/minerals	C, A, E, folate, riboflavin

Melons

Melons include a wide variety and are valued for being relatively low in sugar. Melons are actually members of the cucurbit family of plants (Cucurbitaceae) that also includes cucumbers, pumpkins, squashes and gourds. The seeds of melons can be dried and used as a healthy snack. Melons provide a wealth

Nutrition: Melons are excellent sources of vitamins A, C, B, K and also fibre, magnesium and antioxidants.
Benefits: Aids digestion, reduces inflammation, boosts the immune system and helps keep eyes healthy.

of antioxidants including carotenoids, vitamin C and plenty of minerals such as calcium, potassium, manganese, selenium, magnesium, zinc and copper. Because the nutritional benefits increase as the fruits ripen, it is best to select fully ripened melons to eat.

Melons contain almost no fat and are low in calories, making them an excellent choice for desserts, particularly if you are watching your weight.

Watermelon

Watermelons are rich in lycopene, beta-carotene and vitamin C – all protective, anti-inflammatory nutrients and especially beneficial for skin and eyesight.

- Watermelon contains citrulline, an amino acid that is converted by our kidneys into arginine, which helps to maintain healthy blood pressure and improves blood flow.

Cantaloupe Melon

Cantaloupe melons are also known as rock or Persian melons. They have a sweet flavour and a musky aroma when ripe.

- Cantaloupe are a good source of carotenoids, vitamin C, potassium, a number of B vitamins, vitamin K and fibre, which help to promote a healthy heart, lower inflammation and maintain healthy blood pressure.

Honeydew Melon

Honeydew melons are a popular summer fruit, low in calories and hydrating due to their plentiful water content.

- Honeydew melons are a good source of vitamin C.
- Honeydew provides vitamin B_6 that stimulates the production of serotonin, a neurotransmitter that helps regulate mood and sleep.

Galia Melon

Galia melons are a hybrid cultivar of cantaloupe and honeydew melons.

- Galia melons are high in vitamin C, carotenoids and fibre, which helps digestive health and balances blood sugar levels. Carotenoids are known for their cancer-protective properties.
- A good source of potassium to maintain healthy blood pressure.

Citrus Fruits

Citrus fruits are famous for being high in vitamin C. They also contain lots of antioxidant phytonutrients, which are thought to have anti-cancer properties. Low in sugar (depending on the variety) compared to other fruits and packed with water and fibre, they can satisfy your appetite and help with weight loss.

Nutrition: Citrus fruits contain a range of minerals including potassium, copper, magnesium and selenium. **Benefits:** Helps to keep the heart healthy, supports the immune system and helps to lower cholesterol.

Oranges

A rich source of vitamin C and polyphenols, oranges are a popular fruit throughout the year. One flavanone called hesperidin has been shown to help lower blood pressure. The flavones in the rind are particularly beneficial for lowering cholesterol.

- Oranges contain lots of antioxidants to maintain cardiovascular health, reducing the risk of strokes and certain cancers.

Lemons

Rich in vitamin C, adding lemon juice to meals can help improve the absorption of iron. Lemon juice is often added to hot water and drunk to stimulate digestion and to help detoxify the body.

- The nutrients in lemons are good for immune health, fighting bacterial and viral infections, as well as helping the body's digestive system.

Limes

Limes are an excellent source of vitamin C and, like lemons, contain limonoid compounds, which have been shown to prevent certain cancers.

- Rich in citric acid, limes may help prevent the formation of kidney stones.
- Limes contain hesperidin, making them beneficial for maintaining healthy cholesterol levels.

Why Eat Grapefruit?

Grapefruits are available in red, pink and white varieties. Grapefruit is an excellent source of vitamin C, a vitamin that helps to strengthen the immune system. Red and pink varieties are rich in lycopene, a nutrient that may help men reduce the risk of developing prostate cancer. Lycopene is also important for a healthy skin.

Grapefruit contains pectin, a form of soluble fibre that helps to lower cholesterol and assists digestive health. Grapefruits are also rich in the phytonutrients known as limonoids that are valued for inhibiting tumours and are thought to be helpful in reducing the risk of certain cancers.

Rocket and Orange Salad with Vinaigrette Dressing

LOW CALORIE

Citrus fruits are a delicious addition to salads and this recipe would work equally well with pink grapefruit segments instead of the oranges. The dressing can be prepared in advance and stored in the refrigerator until needed. Add some protein such as cooked chicken or fish to make this a speedy lunch option.

Prep: 10 mins

Ingredients (serves 4)

100 g (3½ oz) rocket, watercress and
    spinach leaves
2 oranges
1 cooked beetroot, sliced
½ red onion, diced
Small handful of flat-leaf parsley, chopped
30 g (1 oz) walnut halves

Vinaigrette Dressing

2 tablespoons sherry vinegar
2 tablespoons walnut oil
2 tablespoons olive oil
Sea salt and freshly ground black pepper

Method

1 Place the rocket, watercress and spinach leaves in a large bowl or serving platter.

2 Using a sharp knife, peel the skin and pith away from the oranges and cut them into segments. Reserve any orange juice that comes out from the fruit.

3 Scatter the beetroot, orange segments, onion, parsley and walnuts over the rocket.

4 Whisk the vinegar and oils with the reserved orange juice and season to taste. Drizzle the vinaigrette dressing over the salad to serve.

KEEPS YOUR HEART HEALTHY	
Calories (per serving)	169
Protein	2.9 g
Total fat	14.5 g
of which saturated fat	1.7 g
Carbohydrates	6.6 g
of which sugars	6.4 g
Vitamins/minerals	C, B, K, A, omega-3 fats

Tropical Fruits

Typically tropical fruits are higher in sugar than other fruits, although this varies depending on the type. Often available frozen, tropical fruits are delicious in a range of both sweet and savoury dishes. Many fruits can also be found in dried form, but choose those without added sugars or additives.

Nutrition: Tropical fruits are full of beneficial vitamins and minerals, as well as antioxidants.
Benefits: Boosts the immune system, aids digestion, helps to keep the skin healthy and boosts your mood.

Papaya

The flesh of papayas is rich orange-pink in colour. The seeds are edible, although their peppery flavour is slightly bitter.

- Papaya contains several unique protein-digesting enzymes that help digestion and reduce inflammation.
- This fruit is a good source of carotenes, vitamin C and flavonoids with immune-supporting benefits.

Pineapple

Pineapple contains bromelain, a digestive enzyme known for its anti-inflammatory and digestive benefits. Eating pineapple may improve digestion of protein foods.

- Pineapple is a good source of the trace mineral manganese and B vitamin thiamin that help boost energy levels.
- This fruit is very rich in vitamin C for immune support and a healthy skin.

Pomegranate

Pomegranate is variously available as fresh fruit, freeze-dried powder or juice.

- Pomegranates are exceptionally rich in vitamin C and high in polyphenols, including ellagic acid, which has been shown to help inhibit cancer cell growth.
- The array of antioxidants present in pomegranates has also been shown to be beneficial to cardiovascular health.

Banana

Popular as a workout fuel, bananas provide easily digestible carbohydrates and potassium to replenish electrolytes lost during exercise. Potassium can also help relieve muscle cramps during workouts.

- Bananas may help lift your mood as they are rich in tryptophan, an amino acid that the body converts to the feel-good neurotransmitter serotonin.

Kiwi Fruit

Packed with more vitamin C than an equivalent quantity of orange, kiwis are a great immune-supporting food.

- Kiwis are rich in vitamin C, which has been shown to help reduce the severity of conditions like osteoarthritis, rheumatoid arthritis and asthma.
- These are high in fibre which can help to remove toxins from the colon.

Chocolate Chip Banana Bread

HEALTHY HEART

A great recipe for a breakfast treat or succulent snack. You can slice and freeze the bread making it a useful standby recipe. It is delicious served on its own or toasted and spread with coconut butter. You could use any nut or seed butter in this recipe.

Prep: 15 mins/Bake: 45 mins

Ingredients (makes 1 loaf)

4 ripe small bananas
4 eggs
100 g (3½ oz) coconut oil
125 g (4½ oz) cashew nut butter
60 g (2 oz) coconut flour
1 teaspoon bicarbonate of soda
2 teaspoons baking powder
1 tablespoon vanilla extract
1 teaspoon ground cinnamon
60 g (2 oz) dairy-free, sugar-free
    chocolate chips

Method

1 Preheat the oven to 180°C (350°F, gas mark 4). Grease a loaf tin and line it with greaseproof paper.

2 Combine the bananas, eggs, oil and nut butter in a food processor. Add the coconut flour, bicarbonate of soda, baking powder, vanilla and cinnamon to the mix and blend them together.

3 Stir in the chocolate chips. Spoon the mixture into the lined loaf tin and bake for 45 minutes until it is golden and cooked through.

4 Cool in the tin for 15 minutes before turning out. Slice the loaf and serve.

PROTEIN PACKED AND HIGH IN FIBRE	
Calories (per slice)	371
Protein	9.1 g
Total fat	28.0 g
of which saturated fat	16.2 g
Carbohydrates	20.2 g
of which sugars	11.0 g
Vitamins/minerals	B, K, potassium, copper

Healthy Fats and Oils

Fats in a Paleo diet are either derived from whole foods such as salmon, meat, nuts and eggs, or from fats used for cooking like coconut oil. Unlike popular low-fat diets, the focus for a Paleo diet is to ensure the consumption of enough quality fats centred around saturated, monounsaturated and omega-3 fats.

Long-chain saturated fatty acids (LCSFA) such as myristic, palmitic and stearic acid are primarily derived from animal fats like lard, duck fat and ghee if dairy is included. These fats form essential components in our cells and are useful for producing energy. They are also heat stable making them suitable for cooking at high temperatures. Saturated fats are in fact very healthy to consume presuming your insulin levels are in a normal range, and there is little evidence that they contribute to heart disease. Some plant-based oils are also great for cooking, such as avocado, palm and coconut oil. Coconut fat is rich in medium-chain triglycerides (MCT). MCTs are metabolized differently from long-chain saturated fats; they don't require bile acids for digestion and they pass directly to the liver for energy conversion. This makes MCTs a great energizing fat.

Monounsaturated fat (MFA), or oleic acid, is found in certain meats, olive oil, avocados, lard and some nuts like macadamia nuts. They are also important structural fats in the body, are heat stable and possess anti-inflammatory properties.

Polyunsaturated fats (PUFA) can be divided into omega-6 and omega-3 types. PUFA are fragile and vulnerable to oxidative damage. Typically the Western diet is very high in omega-6 fats which are pro-inflammatory. Therefore these should only be eaten in small quantities. Cereal grains, some meats and industrial processed and refined oils are also high in omega-6 fats.

Omega-3 fats include alpha-linolenic acid (ALA) and long-chain EPA and DHA fatty acids. They have anti-inflammatory properties. Conversion of ALA is poor so it is important to ensure that we have optimal levels of EPA and DHA which are found in oily fish. Vegetarian sources of omega-3 fats are poorly converted by the body into these active fats.

Health Benefits of Fats and Oils

 Brain health: Your brain is mainly made of cholesterol and fat, most of which are essential fatty acids, in particular DHA. Eating the right fats can therefore improve cognitive function and mood. Medium-chain triglycerides can be used as a fuel by the brain and may help to alleviate cognitive decline.

 Heart health: Healthy fats, including monounsaturated fats, can decrease inflammation, lower circulating triglycerides and reduce insulin due to the natural antioxidants they contain. Saturated fats don't damage easily in high heat, making them the safest fats to cook with because oxidized (damaged) fats cause inflammation in the arteries. Saturated fats can help raise HDL, the 'good' cholesterol that helps to lower your risk of heart disease.

 Immune support: Some fats provide vitamins D and A that are important for immune health, plus the compounds lauric and capryllic acid known to have anti-microbial benefits.

Reproductive health: Fat is critical for reproductive health in both men and women because it is used to manufacture hormones and helps to regulate hormone balance. Healthy fats can also lower inflammation and improve symptoms linked to PMS and the menopause. For men, healthy fats stimulate the production of testosterone.

 Body composition: Including more fat and less carbohydrate in the diet can improve insulin sensitivity, reduce inflammation and support your metabolism.

Duck Fat

Duck fat is primarily composed of long-chain saturated and monounsaturated fats. It has a high smoke point, making it ideal for cooking at very hot temperatures. Duck fat is used in classic dishes and produces delicious crisp roasted vegetables.

- Duck fat is high in monounsaturated fat that can help to lower levels of cholesterol in the blood.

Ghee

Ghee, or clarified butter, is a dietary source of fat traditionally used in Indian cooking. Although not included in all Paleo diets as it is derived from dairy, ghee has a higher smoke point than normal butter, olive oil or coconut oil, making it a great choice for sautéing or frying foods. Because the milk solids have been removed, it's very low in lactose making it acceptable to people with lactose intolerance. Ghee provides butyrate, a short-chain fatty acid that can decrease inflammation and help support colon health.

- Ghee is rich in fat-soluble vitamins A, D, E and K, which are important for bones and brain health, and to boost the immune system.
- Choose ghee from grass-fed cows as it is high in conjugated linoleic acid (CLA) that can improve insulin resistance and encourage healthy body composition.

Lard

Lard is an animal fat normally obtained from pigs. It is high in saturated fat making it very stable for cooking. Choose lard from grass-fed animals for a better fat profile.

- A traditional, sustainable fat, lard provides cholesterol, an important fat needed for hormone production.
- Lard provides vitamin D, an essential vitamin for immunity and bone health.

Avocado Oil

A versatile oil ideal for salad dressings, marinades and high-temperature cooking, avocados are rich in the heart-healthy monounsaturated fat, oleic acid. Oleic acid has been linked to reduced inflammation and may have anti-cancer properties.

- Avocados contain the antioxidants lutein and zeaxanthin, which are important for eye health and lower the risk of macular degeneration and cataracts.

- They are packed with a number of nutrients notably vitamin K, potassium, folate, vitamin E and vitamin C.
- Rich in fibre, avocados can help to balance blood sugar levels and may actually promote weight loss.
- Consuming avocado oil with plant foods can help the body to absorb the fat-soluble vitamins A, E and K and also carotenoids in foods.

Olive Oil

The less refined the oil, the lower the smoking point but higher the antioxidant levels. For lower temperature cooking choose virgin olive oil and for dressings opt for extra virgin olive oil.

- The high monounsaturated fat content of olives has been linked to a reduced risk of cardiovascular disease.
- Olives are rich in phytonutrients.

Walnut Oil

Unrefined walnut oil is made from nuts that are dried and cold pressed. Use in dressings and baking.

- Walnut oil is rich in antioxidants, specifically ellagic acid that has anti-cancer properties.
- This oil contains high levels of monounsaturated oils which are anti-inflammatory and good for the heart.

Macadamia Oil

Macadamia oil is high in monounsaturated fats and is an excellent source of oleic acid. It imparts a mild, buttery flavour to foods making it delicious to use to make mayonnaise. Having a long shelf life, it can be used for low-temperature cooking as well as in dressings.

- Macadamia oil contains vitamin E, a potent fat-protective antioxidant.

Red Palm Oil

Naturally reddish, palm oil is extracted from the flesh of the plum-sized palm fruit. Red palm oil is the virgin unrefined oil. Refined palm oil is a good choice for high-temperature cooking. However, refining the oil reduces its antioxidant content.

- Red palm oil is packed with antioxidants including vitamin E and CoQ10 that is important for energy production.

Why Eat Coconut?

A variety of coconut-derived ingredients – from coconut oil and coconut water to coconut flour and coconut milk – are popular in Paleo diets. Coconut milk is made from a combination of coconut meat and water and is delicious used in sweet and savoury dishes. Coconut water is a great hydrating liquid, rich in electrolytes sodium, potassium and magnesium, making it a popular sports drink. The coconut flesh makes a great snack, low in carbohydrates and very satisfying due to its high fat content.

Coconut oil provides medium-chain triglycerides (MCTs) which are easier to burn as a fuel for the body and the brain. Supplementing with MCT oil has been shown to be beneficial for neurodegenerative conditions such as Alzheimer's. Coconut oil is also rich in lauric acid that boosts immune function and caprylic acid that has anti-microbial properties and may help people with a bacterial or yeast infection. MCTs have also been shown to lower inflammation and support gut barrier healing making them helpful for autoimmune conditions.

Paleo Storecupboard

If you're looking to adopt a Paleo style of eating, then it is worth spending time clearing out your storecupboard and stocking it instead with some healthy Paleo staples.

By restocking your storecupboard with healthy foods, you will have the essentials to create a range of dishes quickly while strengthening your resolve to follow a nutrient-dense diet.

Key products include those for cooking (oils, fats) and baking (coconut flour, almond flour), tinned items (such as tinned fish and coconut milk), drinks (green tea, yerba mate, herbal teas), snacks (nuts, seeds, jerky, seaweed snacks, kale crisps), spices, herbs, flavourings (tamari, coconut aminos, vinegar), sweeteners (honey) and dried goods like sea vegetables and dried mushrooms, etc. These foods are not only convenient but also have numerous health benefits and nutrients to get you in the best of health.

Health Benefits of Storecupboard Staples

 Anti-inflammatory: Many spices, such as turmeric, ginger and garlic, are known for their powerful anti-inflammatory properties making them good for autoimmune conditions. They also benefit cardiovascular health and relieve inflammatory conditions like asthma and arthritis.

 Heart health: Storecupboard ingredients like tinned fish, tinned tomatoes and chocolate contain a range of nutrients that are good for the heart. These include omega-3 fats, antioxidants and magnesium.

Blood sugar: Condiments such as vinegar can lower the blood sugar response after eating, improving insulin function and even your feeling of fullness when taken before or during the meal. Cinnamon is also a beneficial spice for improving blood sugar regulation.

 Digestive health: Some storecupboard ingredients like coconut flour are rich in digestible fibres that encourage bowel regularity and provide prebiotic fibres to boost levels of beneficial bacteria in our gut.

Joint health: Bone broth and gelatine contain a number of nutrients that are beneficial for connective tissues and bone health, including collagen, hyaluronic acid and chondroitin sulphate.

Spices and Flavours

Spices not only add flavour to dishes but they are rich in antioxidants that are known to be good for our health. For those following an autoimmune Paleo diet, certain spices may not be appropriate as they are derived from the nightshade family of plants. These include chillies, paprika and cayenne pepper.

Nutrition: Spices are packed with vitamins, minerals and antioxidants, as well as enhancing the flavour of dishes.
Benefits: Fights infection and boosts the immune system, alleviates nausea, aids digestion and keeps skin healthy.

Ginger

Ginger is the underground rhizome of the ginger plant and is popular in Asian dishes as well as in baking. Known as a carminative spice, it is traditionally used to alleviate digestive disorders, wind and nausea.

- Ginger contains anti-inflammatory compounds called gingerols which may help with inflammatory conditions including arthritis.

Turmeric

Turmeric is the spice that gives curry its yellow colour. Curcumin is the main active ingredient in turmeric. It has powerful anti-inflammatory effects and is a very strong antioxidant.

- Curcumin has been shown to be effective at delaying or even reversing age-related decline in brain function including Alzheimer's disease.

Himalayan Sea Salt

Unlike refined table salt which is chemically cleaned, Himalayan sea salt is unrefined and free of additives.

- Himalayan salt provides a number of trace minerals including potassium, calcium and magnesium that help maintain healthy fluid levels and replenish important electrolytes lost through sweating.

Cinnamon

Cinnamon is the bark of the cinnamon tree. It is available in its dried tubular form, known as a quill, or as ground powder.

- Cinnamon contains a number of volatile oils including cinnamaldehyde. These have anti-microbial benefits, anti-clotting properties and help the body to respond better to insulin so assisting with control of blood sugar levels.

Vanilla

A useful flavouring, vanilla contains chemicals called vanilloids that have anti-inflammatory properties. These are vulnerable to heat so use in cold dishes or in low-temperature baked goods. Most vanilla products are processed, so look for organic vanilla pods or pure extract.

- Traditionally vanilla was used to relieve gastrointestinal symptoms.

Garlic Flakes

Garlic flakes, sometimes called instant garlic, are small dehydrated pieces of garlic that are used as a flavouring. Use them in soups, stews and sauces. Store in an airtight container.

- Garlic can help to lower cholesterol and reduce the risk of heart disease.
- These flakes aid detoxification due to their anti-microbial properties.

Nutritional Yeast Flakes

Nutritional yeast is a rich source of B vitamins and adds a delicious nutty, slightly cheesy flavour to dishes. It is derived from a yeast called *Saccharomyces cerevisiae* and is grown on sugar cane and beet molasses. Once harvested, it undergoes heat treatment and is then crumbled or flaked.

- Nutritional yeast flakes are a source of all essential amino acids and fibre.

Coconut Aminos

Coconut aminos is a soya-free flavouring made from the sap of the coconut tree. Available in health food shops.

- Coconut aminos is especially rich in amino acids that are important for the repair and growth of muscle tissue, keeping the nervous system and brain healthy, as well as aiding digestion and contributing to a healthy heart.

Cashew Nut Cheese

HIGH FIBRE

This is a delicious alternative to dairy cheeses. Using nutritional yeast flakes provides plenty of flavour and also a health-boosting array of B vitamins. Ideally ferment the nut cheese overnight to increase the levels of probiotic bacteria in it. For a quicker option, simply blend all the ingredients together and serve. You can stir in herbs or sun-dried tomato for additional flavour.

**Soak: 8 hrs/Prep: 10 mins/
Stand: 24 hrs**

Ingredients (serves 8)

250 g (9 oz) cashew nuts, soaked overnight
   and drained
250 ml (8 fl oz) water
1 teaspoon probiotic powder
½ teaspoon Himalayan sea salt
1 tablespoon nutritional yeast flakes

Method

1 Blend the nuts, water and probiotic powder in a high-speed liquidizer until the mixture is smooth.

2 Place the mixture in a sieve that has been lined with muslin. Fold the muslin over the top and place a light weight on top. This causes any excess liquid to drain out.

3 Leave to stand for 24 hours. Then stir in the salt and yeast flakes. Store in the refrigerator until ready to use.

CHOLESTEROL FREE AND HEART-HEALTHY	
Calories (per serving)	185
Protein	6.4 g
Total fat	15.1 g
of which saturated fat	3.0 g
Carbohydrates	5.9 g
of which sugars	1.4 g
Vitamins/minerals	B, K, magnesium, zinc

Vinegars and Sauces

Ready-made sauces are not generally used in the Paleo diet as they are made from refined sugars, grains and gluten, but you can use fish sauce, natural oyster sauce and tamari, as well as making your own. Many vinegars are acceptable, including apple cider and balsamic, but malt vinegar contains gluten so should be avoided.

Nutrition: Vinegar contains vitamins, minerals and acetic acid, while fish sauce is rich in iodine.

Benefits: Lowers blood sugar levels after meals, good for keeping the heart healthy and aiding digestion.

Apple Cider Vinegar

Organic, unfiltered apple cider vinegar is rich in acetic acid and contains 'mother' strands of proteins, enzymes and friendly bacteria that cause the cloudy appearance.

- Acetic acid has anti-microbial properties and promotes digestion.
- Apple cider vinegar improves insulin sensitivity and helps to lower blood sugar responses after meals.

Balsamic Vinegar

Choose good-quality balsamic vinegar as cheaper brands often contain sugar and unwelcome additives.

- Balsamic vinegar has been shown to help inhibit LDL oxidation and lipid peroxidation making it beneficial for heart health.
- This vinegar can be helpful in maintaining healthy blood sugar levels.

Red Wine Vinegar

This vinegar is made from red wine that has been fermented for up to two years.

- Red wine vinegar contains acetic acid, which can help curb hunger pangs and aid weight loss as it slows down the digestion process.
- This vinegar contains the antioxidant resveratrol, which can lower blood pressure and keep the heart healthy.

Fish Sauce

Made from small fermented fish, fish sauce is an Asian condiment that adds a distinct flavour as well as salty taste to dishes. Use in small amounts due to its strong flavour.

- Fish sauce contains the vital nutrients and minerals found in fish, but enhanced by fermentation. This includes iodine and other substances that nourish the thyroid, as well as vitamins A and D.

Tamari

Tamari is a Japanese wheat-free fermented soy sauce. It is thicker than ordinary soy sauce and can be used in a variety of savoury dishes to enhance their flavour.

- A good source of manganese to keep bones strong.
- Tamari contains the amino acid tryptophan, which helps reduce sleeping difficulties and boosts your mood.

Flours and Setting Agents

Coconut and other nut flours are very good substitutes for non-Paleo grain and wheat flours. They are also nutritious as they are packed with protein, fibre and healthy fats. You can buy them from health food shops. Gelatine, agar and arrowroot are all useful setting agents that can be used in both desserts and savoury dishes.

Nutrition: Full of fibre and protein, as well as vitamins and minerals, they are all highly nutritious.

Benefits: Improves digestion, keeps skin and hair healthy, helps with weight loss and keeps bones strong.

Coconut Flour

This flour is made from coconut meat that has been dried and defatted. It is valuable for baking Paleo breads, cakes, biscuits, and muffins.

- Coconut flour is relatively low in carbohydrates but high in fibre which contributes to digestive health.
- This flour helps to create a feeling of fullness and balances blood sugar levels.

Almond Flour

Almond flour is highly nutritious, easy to use and readily available. High in protein, low in carbohydrates and low in sugars, it is beneficial for weight loss and improving muscle mass.

- Almond flour is particularly rich in magnesium, phosphorous, potassium and calcium as well as heart-protective vitamin E.

Arrowroot

A useful starch in Paleo cooking obtained from the rootstock of the arrowroot plant; it is dried and then powdered into a flour. Arrowroot can be used to lighten Paleo baking recipes. It is also useful for thickening sauces, both sweet and savoury. Arrowroot is gluten free.

- Arrowroot contains good levels of vitamins, including niacin and thiamin.

Gelatine

Gelatine from grass-fed animals is a nutritious addition to the Paleo diet and can be added to recipes and drinks.

- A great source of collagen, gelatine is also rich in the amino acids glycine and proline and is particularly beneficial for gut healing, the condition of skin, hair and nails and joint and bone health.

Agar Flakes

Derived from seaweed, agar flakes are often used to set liquids and they also act as a binder in recipes. Dissolve agar in boiling liquid for use in a range of dishes.

- Agar contains calcium and iron, and is a good source of fibre.
- This contains no sugar, no fat and no carbohydrates and may help the body to detoxify and aid digestive health.

Why Eat Cacao?

Nutrient-rich cacao has been prized by many cultures for over 2,000 years. But it is important to remember that raw, unsweetened cacao powder and chocolate, which is high in antioxidant flavonols, is very different from the common commercial cocoa drinks and chocolates, which are loaded with sugar and low in antioxidant content.

Cacao is extracted from cacao beans, which are found in the pods (or fruit) of the cacao plant – a tropical tree that is native to Central and South America. Loaded with antioxidants, cacao is also an excellent source of minerals including magnesium, iron, chromium, manganese, zinc and copper. It is one of the richest food sources of magnesium, which helps to relax the muscles and heart and cardiovascular system and relieve stress. Many of the health benefits appear to be due to the antioxidant content, so choose raw cacao powder for optimal benefits.

Cacao also contains the amino acid tryptophan and phenylethylamine (PEA), which has a positive effect on mood. Raw cacao powder is milder in flavour than commercial roasted cocoa powder. Processed chocolate powders generally lack many of the health benefits of the raw ingredient.

In addition to cacao powder, you can also find cacao nibs, cacao butter and paste. Cacao nibs are slightly bitter and have a strong chocolate flavour. Cacao butter and paste are popular in raw desserts and for making home-made chocolates.

Although chocolate can be a healthy food option it is still energy dense and so will make you gain weight if you eat too much of it. Dark chocolate has been shown to offer a number of health benefits including improving blood pressure and blood flow, which may be one of the reasons it can support cognitive function. Choose dark chocolate containing 85 per cent cocoa solids for a higher intake of beneficial antioxidants and lower sugar content.

Berry Jellies with Coconut Yogurt

STRONG BONES

A simple light dessert made using grass-fed gelatine. You can use any berries, and bags of frozen berries are a great standby option if fresh are not available. By puréeing the berries, you create a more intense, thicker set jelly than by simply using juice. Instead of coconut yogurt, you could top the jellies with coconut cream.

Prep: 15 mins/Chill: 3 to 4 hrs

Ingredients (serves 2)

150 g (5 oz) strawberries

130 g (4½ oz) raspberries

2 tablespoons grass-fed gelatine powder

250 ml (8 fl oz) water or pomegranate juice

Method

1 Purée the fruit in a liquidizer. Place the gelatine in a pan and mix in the fruit purée and water or juice. Stir well.

2 Bring the liquid to the boil stirring constantly to dissolve the gelatine. Leave the mixture to cool.

3 Pour into glasses or bowls. Place in the refrigerator to set for 3–4 hours. Top with coconut yogurt or cream and a few berries to serve.

BOOSTS YOUR SKIN, HAIR AND NAILS	
Calories (per serving)	144
Protein	8.8 g
Total fat	9.3 g
of which saturated fat	6.6 g
Carbohydrates	7.5 g
of which sugars	7.1 g
Vitamins/minerals	C, K, manganese

Creamy Coconut Chocolate Mousse

ENERGIZING

A rich, creamy mousse that makes an unashamedly indulgent treat. You can also turn this into a frozen dessert by spooning it into freezer-proof moulds. The addition of cacao butter or coconut oil helps to set the mousse and gives it a rich flavour.

Prep: 10 mins/Chill: 3 to 4 hrs

Ingredients (serves 2)

1 x 400 g (14 oz) can coconut milk
2 tablespoons cashew or almond
   nut butter
2 tablespoons coconut oil or cacao
   butter, melted
Pinch of ground cinnamon
100 g (3½ oz) honey
30 g (1 oz) raw cacao powder

Method

1 Simply place all the ingredients in a liquidizer or food processor and process until smooth.

2 Pour into glasses or ramekins and place in the refrigerator for 3–4 hours to harden. Alternatively, place in the freezer for 1 hour to set. Top with berries and a sprig of mint to serve.

BURSTING WITH ANTIOXIDANTS	
Calories (per serving)	239
Protein	3.2 g
Total fat	12.3 g
of which saturated fat	7.8 g
Carbohydrates	28.5 g
of which sugars	23.3 g
Vitamins/minerals	E, iron, calcium, copper

Fermented Foods

The traditional diet of every ancient culture contained foods that were fermented. Originally this was done primarily to preserve food for longer, but we now know that it also creates very healthy, easily digested foods that are rich in probiotics.

Fermented foods are foods that have been through a process called lactofermentation where natural bacteria and yeasts from the surrounding environment – and on the vegetables and fruit themselves – feed on the sugar and starch contained in the foods to

create lactic acid. This anaerobic process (fermentation) does more than just preserve the food, however, it also makes the nutrients inside the food easier to digest and more bioavailable. For example, the amount of bioavailable vitamin C in sauerkraut is 20 times higher than in the same helping of fresh cabbage. This is because in the fresh cabbage vitamin C is bound in the cellulose structure, which can be more difficult to digest and so absorb. As communities of specific health-promoting bacteria grow, they consume sugars and produce valuable enzymes. Fermented foods provide you with a beneficial bacteria to strengthen your immune and digestive systems.

Cultures all over the world have been eating fermented foods for a long time, from Sauerkraut (see page 188) in Germany to kimchi (see page 184) in Korea.

Left: Kimchi is a traditional Korean fermented dish believed to slow down ageing. It is made from vegetables, including cabbage and spices.

Health Benefits of Fermented Foods

 Lower inflammation: Fermented foods can have anti-inflammatory properties making them useful for conditions such as asthma and respiratory infections.

 Immune health: Probiotic bacteria are known to strengthen immune function making them beneficial for autoimmune conditions. Some, such as kefir, also provide a wealth of amino acids that are important for immune function.

 Digestive health: Fermented foods are rich in probiotic bacteria that help digestion. This enables you to digest fats, proteins and carbohydrates more easily, as well as giving support to the gut barrier lining. They are particularly beneficial to take after antibiotics to reinoculate the gut flora.

 Child health: Probiotic bacteria are particularly important for supporting a child's digestive system, which is not fully mature. As fermented foods are pre-digested, it is easier for children to assimilate the valuable nutrients from them.

Urinary health: The beneficial yeasts and bacteria in fermented foods can help to fight infections in the urinary tract, which are typically caused by an overgrowth of pathogenic bacteria.

Kimchi

This is a popular Korean fermented food. While recipes vary, it normally contains fermented cabbage, radish and other vegetables as well as spices including garlic and chilli. It is popular served with spicy beef dishes.

- Kimchi is a good source of vitamins A, C and B vitamins and its probiotic 'healthy bacteria' aids digestion.

Why Eat Kefir?

An ancient cultured food, kefir is a fermented milk drink. It is rich in amino acids, enzymes, calcium, magnesium, phosphorus and B vitamins. Kefir contains several strains of friendly bacteria as well as beneficial yeasts, which can support digestive function and immune health. It is made with kefir 'grains', which are not actually a grain but are a mother culture of bacteria and yeasts. Although cow's milk is typically used, it can also be made with sheep's milk, coconut or nut milk. You can also make water kefir using water grains.

You can purchase kefir in health food shops or make it at home using kefir grains and either organic dairy milk or coconut milk. It takes between 24 and 30 hours to ferment the cultures in milk at room temperature. Once fermented, store the kefir in the refrigerator and consume it within four days. Since the kefir grains react with metals, do not use any metal utensils when preparing. If making coconut milk kefir, you will need to refresh the kefir grains in cow's milk after four to five batches to enable it to ferment.

Home-made Coconut Kefir

PROTEIN RICH

One of the most healthy fermented foods, you can make your own effervescent kefir as a tangy, fresh and tasty alternative to yogurt.

Prep: 20 mins/Ferment: 24 hrs

Ingredients (serves 4)

1 sachet of milk kefir grains
1 litre (35 fl oz) organic whole coconut milk

You need a clean, sterilized jar big enough to hold 1 litre (35 fl oz).

Method

1 Place the kefir in a small sterilized glass jar and pour over the coconut milk. Stir well with a wooden spoon. Cover with a lid or cloth and ferment in a warm place, away from direct sunlight, for at least 24 hours. Do not seal the lid, as gas can build up as the mixture ferments.

2 The milk will separate to form the kefir liquid at the bottom. Carefully pour the mixture through a fine sieve and collect the kefir liquid in a clean container.

3 Store the prepared kefir in the refrigerator until required.

4 After straining, the grains should be placed straight back into a clean jar without washing them first. Fresh coconut milk is added to the grains to make the next batch of kefir.

AIDS DIGESTION	
Calories (per serving)	70
Protein	1 g
Total fat	6 g
of which saturated fat	5 g
Carbohydrates	6 g
of which sugars	3 g
Vitamins/minerals	A, C, calcium, iron

Sauerkraut

Sauerkraut is based on shredded cabbage but may also include other vegetables, such as carrot. If purchasing sauerkraut, choose an organic raw brand as many commercial brands will be heat-treated and lack any beneficial bacteria.

- Based on cabbage it provides plenty of vitamin C, vitamin K and fibre.

Kombucha

Kombucha was called the 'immortal health elixir' by the ancient Chinese and it has been consumed for more than 2,000 years. It is made from sweetened tea that has been fermented by a symbiotic colony of bacteria and yeast (known as SCOBY).

- Kombucha is rich in enzymes that your body requires for digestion and encourages blood cleansing.

Soured Cream

Soured cream is simply fermented cream. For a non-dairy version, simply chill a tin of coconut milk for an hour, then open the tin without shaking it, scoop out the hard cream on top, put in a bowl, stir well until creamy and add 2 tablespoons white vinegar, then chill before serving.

- Soured cream contains calcium and phosphorous to keep bones healthy.

Yogurt

A popular traditional food, yogurt is typically made from dairy ingredients. Many people on a Paleo diet avoid all dairy products including sheep and goat's milk, but yogurt can be made easily from coconut or nut milks.

■ Coconut yogurt contains beneficial bacteria, fibre, vitamins and minerals, to aid digestion and prevent constipation.

Home-made Coconut Yogurt   ANTI-AGEING

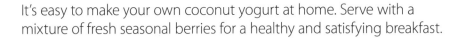

It's easy to make your own coconut yogurt at home. Serve with a mixture of fresh seasonal berries for a healthy and satisfying breakfast.

Prep: 30 mins/Ferment: 8 to 12 hrs

Ingredients (serves 4)

2 x 400 g (14 fl oz) cans organic whole
   coconut milk
1 tablespoon agar flakes or 2 teaspoons
   gelatine
1 tablespoon yogurt or 1 pack of yogurt
   starter or 1 teaspoon probiotic powder

Method

1 Place the coconut milk and agar flakes in a saucepan and simmer, stirring until the agar has dissolved. Remove from the heat and cool to room temperature.

2 Add the yogurt starter and stir thoroughly. Pour the mixture into a yogurt maker and ferment for 8–12 hours. Or pour into a clean jar, cover and ferment at 43°C (110°F). Stir well and put the yogurt in the refrigerator to thicken.

SUPPORTS THE IMMUNE SYSTEM	
Calories (per serving)	199
Protein	1.7 g
Total fat	18.7 g
of which saturated fat	16 g
Carbohydrates	7.2 g
of which sugars	1.6 g
Vitamins/minerals	A, B, C, D, calcium, iron

Sauerkraut

LOW CALORIE

Unlike many shop-bought versions, home-made sauerkraut is raw and therefore richer in beneficial enzymes and probiotic bacteria. Use organic, fresh vegetables and wash and dry them thoroughly. You can vary the vegetables according to taste. This version includes carrots and onions for additional flavour and beneficial nutrients.

Prep: 8 hrs 30mins/
Ferment: 3 to 4 days

Ingredients (serves around 10)

1 cabbage e.g. Savoy, thinly sliced
3 carrots, grated or finely chopped
2 shallots, finely chopped
2 tablespoons sea salt
125 ml (4 fl oz) warm water
2 garlic cloves, peeled and chopped
1 teaspoon caraway seeds
2 teaspoons fennel seeds
Handful of washed, soaked sea vegetables
    chopped, optional

BOOSTS YOUR IMMUNE SYSTEM	
Calories (per serving)	25
Protein	2.0 g
Total fat	0 g
of which saturated fat	0 g
Carbohydrates	4.0 g
of which sugars	1.0 g
Vitamins/minerals	C, K, B₆, sodium, folate

Method

1 Place the vegetables in a large mixing bowl. Put the salt and water in a separate small bowl and stir to dissolve. Pour over the vegetables and massage the mixture with your hands. Leave at room temperature to soften overnight.

2 The following day, drain and reserve the salt water. Stir the garlic, caraway and fennel seeds into the cabbage mixture and add the sea vegetables, if you are using them. Mix well. Tightly pack the mixture into a large glass jar with a lid. Pour over the saved salt water and press it firmly so there is no trapped air inside and the cabbage is covered in its own juice. Close the lid tightly.

3 Leave the jar in a warm, dark place for 3–4 days. It will take at least a week to ferment if left in a cool place. When ready, store in the refrigerator until required.

Beverages

The most important beverage that your body needs is water. Water makes up about 60 per cent of the human body and plays a key role in all our physiological processes.

For many people who switch to a Paleo style of eating, making a change from their favourite drinks can be difficult. Whether you've been used to consuming energy drinks, beers or fizzy drinks, there are healthier alternatives that will not only hydrate the body but also provide refreshment and, in some cases, bring you additional health benefits. If you already eat a large variety of vegetables, then some water will be delivered from the food that you consume.

Remember that many of the fermented products previously discussed are also drinks – kombucha, water kefir and milk kefir are recommended.

Water is the primary drink in the Paleo lifestyle. If you find plain water boring, try sparkling water or add a squeeze of lime or lemon for an extra kick. Just by adding various flavourings to plain water you may find that you drink more. Cucumber slices, mint and lemon wedges in water are also refreshing. Some people like to add a splash of apple cider vinegar to warm water to drink before meals to stimulate digestion.

If you are taking strenuous exercise, consider adding lemon juice to water plus a pinch of salt. Lemons are high in potassium and the salt will help replace sodium lost when you sweat.

It is not a good idea to drink fruit juice because of its high sugar content. Green juices and smoothies, however, are beneficial, especially if you are looking for an opportunity to include a wider variety and quantity of vegetables in your diet and find eating larger amounts of vegetables difficult to achieve.

Health Benefits of Beverages

Brain health: Dehydration can affect our cognitive function. It may impair your attention span, memory and motor skills. Drinking enough water will keep you feeling alert, allowing you to function optimally and it can also help to relieve migraines.

Energy: Water is needed by our cells to function efficiently. Even minor dehydration can lead to low energy levels and fatigue. Drinks rich in electrolytes can replenish flagging energy while others that contain caffeine provide a more instant lift. Certain herbal teas like ginseng or liquorice are adrenal adaptogens, which can also be effective energy boosters.

Weight loss: Drinking water before and between meals helps you to feel full, meaning you are likely to eat less. Many people mistake hunger for thirst so if you feel hungry, first drink a glass of water. Other drinks like green tea have also been shown to stimulate fat burning and aid weight loss.

Digestive health: Drinking enough water prevents constipation and supports kidney and liver function by helping to flush away waste products. In the large intestine, water binds with fibre to increase the bulk of the stools, reduce transit time and make defecation easier.

Skin health: For glowing skin it is important to drink enough water. It assists cell health, lubricates the body and by helping excretion of toxins may keep your skin looking clear.

Tea

Tea contains far less caffeine than coffee, but black tea tends to have more caffeine than green or white tea. If you want to avoid caffeine altogether, drink herbal teas.

■ Green and black tea both provide a variety of health benefits including having antioxidant, anti-carcinogenic and anti-inflammatory properties.

Herbal Teas

Herbal teas are delicious served either hot or cold. Made from herbs or fruit extracts, some have specific health benefits.

■ For a calming tea before bedtime try valerian, camomile or lemon balm. Other teas can help to maintain a healthy gut, such as mint, ginger, turmeric or marshmallow root.

Green Tea

Available as loose leaf, teabags or green tea matcha powder, which is the whole leaf ground up. The health benefits of matcha tea exceed those of green tea infusions.

■ Green tea is rich in catechins, particularly EGCG which is a powerful antioxidant with anti-cancer benefits. Green tea has been shown to boost the metabolic rate and increase fat burning.

Rooibos Tea

Rooibos tea or red bush comes from a South African bush. It is caffeine free.

- Rooibos is rich in antioxidants including polyphenols, which have anti-inflammatory and anti-cancer properties. It contains quercetin known for its anti-inflammatory benefits, particularly for conditions such as asthma and for settling digestive upsets.

Coffee

Coffee occupies a bit of a grey area in the Paleo diet. While it was not an ancestral food, scientific research suggests that it can be beneficial to health when it is well tolerated. Some people do not metabolize it well and it can cause adverse effects.

There is concern that high coffee consumption may increase intestinal permeability, which is why it is often limited or avoided on an autoimmune protocol. Its caffeine content can adversely affect the adrenal glands by stimulating them to release the stress hormones cortisol and adrenaline, which is the same as the fight or flight response and over time this can lead to adrenal fatigue. High cortisol levels may also interfere with sleep, impair digestion and overstimulate the immune system.

- Coffee is rich in antioxidants and polyphenols, and a number of studies have shown a range of health benefits including prevention of cancer, diabetes, cardiovascular disease, Alzheimer's and Parkinson's disease.

- Coffee can aid weight loss due to antioxidants present including chlorogenic and caffeic acids which appear to curb overeating and reduce body fat. Unroasted coffee is richer in antioxidants and has been studied for its contribution to weight loss.

Maple Water

Maple water is liquid extracted from maple trees. It is a sweet, naturally filtered water, which contains a number of minerals such as calcium, potassium, magnesium and manganese, which can be good for the heart and kidneys.

- Slightly lower in sugar than coconut water, maple water contains enzymes, which help digestion and excretion.

Birch Water

Similar to maple water, this drink comes from tapping a birch tree. Birch water is often flavoured. It also contains electrolytes and aids detoxification and cleansing due to its diuretic properties.

- Birch water contains saponin, which helps to promote healthy cholesterol levels.
- Birch water contains xylitol, a sugar alcohol that helps prevent tooth decay.

Coconut Water

Coconut water is a natural isotonic drink that provides the same energy-boosting benefits as formulated sports drinks.

- Coconut water is rich in the electrolytes calcium, magnesium, phosphorus, sodium and potassium, which are rapidly absorbed and assimilated by the body. It can help maintain healthy blood pressure.

Juices Versus Smoothies

Fruit juices are not recommended due to their high sugar content. Green juices and smoothies can be a valuable addition to a Paleo diet as a way of increasing vegetable intake. Green juices lack fibre, which makes vitamins, minerals and antioxidants more easily absorbed, but can unbalance blood sugar levels as fibre helps to slow down the absorption of sugars. To avoid this, consume a green juice with a meal or limit the portion size.

Incorporating green juices can help people who have digestive problems and find it difficult to digest cooked or raw vegetables. To keep the sugar content low, make your juices using vegetables rather than fruit and try lifting the taste with a little lemon or ginger. You can add one green apple if you find that vegetable green juices taste too bitter.

Green smoothies – where the ingredients are simply blended together with water or another liquid – do contain fibre and are often more satisfying. This is an effective way to increase your intake of vegetables easily without putting a strain on your digestion. They are a useful way to sneak in various supplements and foods such as collagen powder, green superfoods, oils, nuts, seeds or protein powders. Often green smoothies contain fruit, so it is important to keep an eye on the sugar content. Green smoothies can be an easy way to start the day if you find breakfast too difficult to manage. To make it more sustaining consider adding some soaked nuts, kefir and dairy-free yogurt. This will help to balance your blood sugar levels.

Why Drink Bone Broth?

Bone broth is an important nutrient-rich food to include in a Paleo diet. Making your own is extremely cost effective, as you can make use of leftover carcass bones that would otherwise be thrown away.

Bone broth is simply made by slowly simmering the bones in water for several hours. To extract as many nutrients as possible, it is a good idea to cut or break up the bones before cooking. When the bone broth is ready, the bones should be strained and discarded. The resulting broth can be stored in the refrigerator for two to three days for use as a drink or added to soups, stews and casseroles. It can also be frozen. When making bone broth, it is important to select bones from organic grass-fed animals for optimal nourishment.

- Home-made bone broth is excellent for speeding healing and recuperation from illness. Chicken broth, for example, contains a natural amino acid called cysteine, which can thin mucus, making it useful for respiratory infections.
- Bone broth is rich in a number of nutrients that are important for healthy bones, including calcium, magnesium and phosphorous.
- Bone broth contains plenty of amino acids such as glycine, proline and arginine which all have anti-inflammatory effects.
- Popular for its role in contributing to a healthy gut, bone broth can assist the healing of the gut lining.
- The gelatine content in bone broth promotes healthy hair, nails and joints and also helps to maintain healthy connective tissues.

Nut and Seed Milks

Nut and seed milks are a valuable addition to a Paleo diet to replace dairy. Many can be purchased ready made but it is also simple to make your own. Commercial brands often contain added sugars and thickeners like guar gum, which some people may find difficult to digest. Almond milk and coconut milk are popular for recipes or used as a dairy alternative in drinks.

- Coconut milk is a staple fat option for those following a Paleo diet.
- Almond milk is a good source of heart-protective vitamin E as well as calcium, to strengthen bones.

Home-made Coconut Milk

HIGH FIBRE

Coconut milk is very easy to make at home. If storing in the refrigerator it may separate, so just give it a quick stir until mixed and then it's ready to use.

Prep: 20 mins

Ingredients (serves 2)

500 ml (18 fl oz) water
90 g (3¼ oz) unsweetened coconut flakes

ANTI-FUNGAL AND ANTIBACTERIAL	
Calories (per serving)	231
Protein	1.6 g
Total fat	16.3 g
of which saturated fat	14.6 g
Carbohydrates	21.1 g
of which sugars	0 g
Vitamins/minerals	D, B12, calcium, iron

Method

1 Heat the water until hot but not boiling. Put the coconut and water in a high-speed liquidizer. Blend on high until thick and creamy.

2 Line a colander or sieve with muslin or use a nut bag and strain the liquid. The coconut pulp can be dried and used in other recipes.

3 You can drink the coconut milk immediately or store it in the refrigerator for two to three days.

Matcha Green Smoothie

WEIGHT LOSS

This amazing creamy smoothie is sweet and nourishing. Studies have shown that exercising after drinking matcha tea can encourage fat burning even more, making this an excellent pre-workout drink. Add a scoop of protein powder if you want to boost the protein content.

Prep: 5 mins

Ingredients (serves 1)

3 Brazil nuts

250 ml (8 fl oz) almond milk or coconut milk

150 g (5 oz) pineapple, fresh or frozen

2 handfuls of kale or spinach

¼ teaspoon matcha green tea powder

1 scoop of protein powder, optional

Method

1 Simply place all the ingredients in a high-speed liquidizer and process until the mixture is smooth and creamy. Pour into a glass and serve.

BOOSTS YOUR BRAIN AND BURNS OFF FAT	
Calories (per serving)	208
Protein	5.4 g
Total fat	9.9 g
of which saturated fat	1.8 g
Carbohydrates	24.8 g
of which sugars	15.1 g
Vitamins/minerals	E, C, B, selenium

Alcohol in the Paleo Diet

Many people following a strict Paleo diet consider that moderate alcohol consumption is consistent with the health goals that the diet promotes.

While some people may benefit from drinking regular, small amounts, alcohol can also be bad for your health in various ways. It is a known irritant to the gut and can cause an increase in intestinal permeability. For this reason,

it is not recommended for people with autoimmune conditions where gut healing is required.

Alcohol is detoxified by the body in the liver, via an enzyme called alcohol dehydrogenase. In some people the activity of this enzyme is reduced which can mean that alcohol is not well tolerated and this can result in more extreme hangovers.

Drinking too much alcohol can also lead to weight gain, high blood sugar and insulin problems, a fatty liver, elevated levels of fats in the blood and homocysteine (an amino acid found in the blood and, if levels become too high, there is an increased risk of heart disease). It can also lead to increased oxidative stress. Alcohol also burdens the digestive and detoxification systems. It can lead to disturbed sleep and is addictive.

Red wine has been associated with some cardiovascular health benefits probably because of the antioxidants it contains. Alcohol in small amounts may help people to unwind and socialize – all of which can be beneficial to health.

If you want to drink alcohol, do so in moderation. Aim for no more than one small glass a day and have regular days which are alcohol free.

Paleo Dos and Don'ts

What to Include

- Grass-fed red meats
- Wild game
- Organ meats
- Offal
- Grass-fed/organic poultry
- Eggs
- Fish
- Shellfish and seafood
- Leafy green vegetables
- Salad vegetables
- Non-starchy vegetables: avocado, olives, etc.
- Allium vegetables: onion, leek, chive, garlic, etc.
- Starchy vegetables: sweet potato, squashes, carrot, beetroot, parsnip, etc.
- Sea vegetables
- Nuts
- Seeds
- Fresh fruits: berries, stone fruits, melons, citrus, apples, pears, tropical fruits, etc.
- Quality fats and oils: lard, duck fat, tallow, red palm oil, olive, walnut, flaxseed, macadamia, avocado, coconut, etc.
- Storecupboard items: gelatine, agar flakes, coconut flour, almond flour, tamari, coconut aminos, nutritional yeast flakes, green banana flour, coconut milk and cream, tinned fish, fish sauce,

tapioca starch, arrowroot, vinegar, cacao powder, carob powder, capers, gherkins, bicarbonate of soda, baking powder, Himalayan sea salt, etc.
- Herbs and spices
- Honey and other sweeteners: stevia, coconut sugar, xylitol if tolerated
- Fermented foods: kefir, sauerkraut, kombucha, etc.
- Beverages: water, herbal teas, green and black tea, coffee (in moderation), green juices and smoothies, coconut water, nut and seed milks, kombucha, kefir, bone broth, stocks, lemon or lime water
- Alcohol (occasionally).

What to Avoid

- Grains: including gluten and non-gluten grains (wheat, spelt, rye, barley, kamut, couscous, semolina, oats, corn, quinoa, rice, amaranth, millet, buckwheat, teff, wild rice, sorghum and products containing these grains)
- Beans and pulses (including peanuts and soya)
- Soya products: soyaflour, soya milk and yogurt, tempeh, tofu, textured vegetable protein, okara, MSG, soya protein, edamame beans
- Dairy products: hard and soft cheeses, ghee, cottage cheese, curds, milk, yogurt, butter, ice cream, soured cream, buttermilk, foods containing dairy and lactose, whey protein powder
- Processed fatty meats (hot dogs, etc.)
- Soft drinks, fizzy drinks and fruit juice
- Sugars, syrups and artificial sweeteners such as aspartame and saccharin
- Processed foods and ready meals
- Refined vegetable oils
- Milk chocolate, white chocolate and sweets
- Refined table salt.

Glossary

Amino acids – these are the building blocks of muscle-building protein. They carry out important functions, have a key role in the storage of nutrients and help in wound healing.

Antioxidants – these protect our bodies against the damaging effects of free radicals. Vitamins C, E, beta-carotene and selenium are antioxidants.

Beta-carotene – a pigment found in large quantities in orange-fleshed and dark green fruit and vegetables and is turned into vitamin A by the body.

Fats – compounds of carbon, hydrogen and oxygen atoms that exist in chains of varying lengths, shapes and orders. They are one of the vital nutrients required by the body for both energy and the construction and maintenance of 'structural' elements, such as cell membranes.

Free radical – a highly chemically reactive molecule often containing oxygen that can cause damage to cells in the body.

Gluten – a group of proteins found in wheat and other cereal grains. Coeliac

disease is a disorder in which the body becomes intolerant to gluten.

Glycaemic index (GI) – rates ingredients and dishes according to the rate at which a carbohydrate food breaks down into sugars and enters the bloodstream.

Glycaemic load (GL) – this estimates how much the food will raise the person's blood sugar level after eating it.

Intestinal barrier – the lining of the intestines, often referred to as the gut barrier or mucosal barrier. It provides a physical barrier between the insides of the gut and the inside of the body.

Intestinal permeability – or leaky gut, this refers to a measure of how permeable the gut lining is. If the gut is compromised, substances that should not cross the barrier are able to do so.

Lectins – a group of carbohydrate-binding proteins found in many foods that can bind to specific carbohydrates including membranes in the gut.

Monounsaturated fat – these fatty acids contain just one double bond in their fatty acid chain. The more double bonds a fatty acid boasts, the more 'fluid' it is. They are generally liquid at room temperature.

Polyunsaturated fats – these fats have more than one double bond in their fatty acid chain. They tend to be liquid even when refrigerated. They include omega-3 and 6 fatty acids.

Prebiotics – non-digestible food ingredients (for example, inulin and certain fibres) that promote the growth of beneficial micro-organisms in the intestines.

Probiotics – beneficial micro-organisms that live in the body, primarily in the gastrointestinal tract.

Saturated fats – these fats have all available carbon bonds paired with hydrogen atoms. They are solid at room temperature.

Index

Credits

Picture credits
(t)= top, (c)= centre, (b)= bottom

Shutterstock.com: 7 sarsmis; 8-9 TDway; 10 Anna Hoychuk; 11 baranq; 12 MaraZe; 16 michaeljung; 17 BlueSkyImage; 19 Stephen VanHorn; 21 Valery Bareta; 23 YuliaKotina; 24 zoryanchik; 27 ElenaGaak; 29 nevodka; 33 Rido; 34-35 amenic181; 36 Subbotina Anna; 38 Anna Hoychuk; 39(t) Anna Hoychuk; 39(c) stockcreations; 39(b) msheldrake; 41 MSPhotographic; 42(c) Sergiy Zavgorodny; 42(b) MSPhotographic; 43(t) Milarka; 43(c) Viktor1; 43(b) svry; 45 Fanfo; 46 Michael Vesia; 47(t) margouillat photo; 47(c) Gayvoronskaya_Yana; 47(b) HLPhoto; 48 NinaM; 49 Anna_Pustynnikova; 51(t) Josef Hanus; 51(c) Wollertz; 51(b) Arsti; 53 Digivic; 54(c) Valerio Pardi; 54(b) HLPhoto; 55(t) Shaiith; 55(c) Jacques Palut; 55(b) Agnes Kantaruk; 57 stockcreations; 59(c) Dani Vincek; 59(b) Paul Cowan; 60(t) sarsmis; 60(c) svry; 60(b) Lesya Dolyuk; 61(t) Bildagentur Zoonar GmbH; 61(c) Otokimus; 61(b) Elena Fabbrili; 63 Africa Studio; 64 Ingrid Balabanova; 65(t) Kalavati; 65(b) zoryanchik; 66 amenic181; 68(c) Jacek Chabraszewski; 68(b) MaraZe; 69(t) Anna Hoychuk; 69(c) Elena Shashkina; 69(b) B. and E. Dudzinscy; 71 Peteer; 72 Dar1930; 73(t) Filipe B. Varela; 73(c) Visionsi; 73(b) Marina Onokhina; 75 Cristi Lucaci; 76(c) svry; 76(b) margouillat photo; 77 Jill Chen; 79 karelnoppe; 80(c) PHB.cz (Richard Semik); 80(b) Lilyana Vynogradova; 81(t) Gayvoronskaya_Yana; 81(c) Pawel Strykowski; 81(b) Robin Stewart; 83 sarsmis; 84 Gayvoronskaya_Yana; 86(t) Kentaro Foto; 86(c) Dream79; 86(b) pixfly; 87 Karpenkov Denis; 89 Bloor; 90 Natalia Van Doninck; 92 Lukas Gojda; 94(c) Dani Vinceks; 94(b) Alexander Raths; 95(t) Zaira Zarotti; 95(c) DJ Srki; 95(b) Troyker; 96(t) Dani Vincek; 96(c) Anna Hoychuk; 96(b) Viktory Panchenko; 97 Aneta_Gu; 99 Kondor83; 100 Photosiber; 101(t) Angorius; 101(b) Anna Hoychuk; 102(c) Dream79; 102(b) ilolab; 103(t) Olga Lyubkina; 103(c) artemisphoto; 103(b) gori910; 105 Shaiith; 106 yonibunga; 108(c) Brent Hofacker; 108(b) B. and E. Dudzinscy; 109(t) Charlotte Lake; 109(c) Elena Shashkina; 109(b) Yevgeniya Shal; 110(t) Andrii Opanasenko; 110(c) Brent Hofacker; 110(b) peuceta; 111(t) Brent Hofacker; 111(b) Tim UR; 113 Brent Hofacker; 114 stockcreations; 115 Tim UR; 116 Kati Molin; 117(t) pilipphoto; 117(c) Dani Vincek; 117(b) zhekoss; 118(c) Viktor1; 118(b) Gayvoronskaya_Yana; 119(t) Quanthem; 119(c) Chamille White; 119(b) Space Monkey Pics; 120(c) bitt24; 120(b) sarsmis; 121(t) Dream79; 121(c) Olha Afanasieva; 121(b) Handmade-Pictures; 123 pearl7; 124(c) Orlio; 124(b) Magdalena Kucova; 125(t) sarsmis; 125(c) DarZel; 125(b) Svetlana Foote; 127 PG Studija; 128(c) jreika; 128(b) yasuhiro amano; 129(t) Madlen; 129(c) Only Fabrizio; 129(b) Miyuki Satake; 131 Mr. Suttipon Yakham; 132 Brent Hofacker; 134(c) Gayvoronskaya_Yana; 134(b) Sea Wave; 135(t) Gayvoronskaya_Yana; 135(c) Diana Taliun; 135(b) marekuliasz; 136(t) Diana Taliun; 136(c) Gayvoronskaya_Yana; 136(b) Christian Jung; 137(c) Gayvoronskaya_Yana; 137(b) tharamust; 138(t) Elena Elisseeva; 138(c) Sea Wave; 138(b) HandmadePictures; 140 Yulia Davidovich; 142(c) HandmadePictures; 142(b) Dionisvera; 143(t) Volosina; 143(c) matka_Wariatka; 143(b) Wiktory; 144 Dionisvera; 145 Liv friis-larsen; 146(c) HandmadePictures; 146(b) nookieme; 147(t) id-art; 147(c) guentermanaus; 147(b) gresei; 148(c) sarsmis; 148(b) Wiktory; 149(c) Orlio;

More About the Author

Christine Bailey
www.christinebailey.co.uk

Christine is a member of the British Association for Applied Nutrition and Nutritional Therapy (BANT), Complementary and Natural Healthcare Council (CNHC) and the NHS Directory of Complementary Therapists. Christine adheres to the strict BANT Code of Ethics and Practice.